We are gateful to
Hannah Werblan-Jakubiec at the University of Warsaw;
Frantisek Kadlec Director at Prague Castle, Jiri Setlik cultural affairs for
Czechoslovakia and Jindrich Chmelar in Brno;
Krisztina Balonyi Hillier, Janos Gerle and Karoly Orsi in Budapest;
Bato and Madge Tomasevic in Belgrade; Gigi Mihaija at the Brancusi Foundation.
Our most sincere thanks go to
The controlling foundations and their directors without
whose kind involvement this project would not have been possible.
We received the most valuable assistance from
Nicola Gordon Bowe, Frances-Jane French, John Gilmartin, Gabor Kende,
Witold Schoenberg in Dublin;
The Friends of Marquand Park in Princeton, Champe Smith in New York.
We thank Sally Prideaux and Cristina Gaspar for their editorial assistance.

Project directed by
M. T. Train

Dersign and production by
B2 Atelier de Design:
José Brandão/Nuno Vale Cardoso

Additional photography
Courtesy of:

Mary Jay Rutherford Collection,
Architectural Slide Library, University of California, Berkely
pages, 79, 95, 202, 203, 204, 205 (lower)

Helen Gabriel
pages 97, (lower) 98, (right), 106, 107, 115, 125, 149, (lower), 150, 151

Hungarian National Museum
pages 143, 152

Caire Milonas
pages 148, 149 (upper)

Janos Huschit and Hillier Zoltanne
pages 153, (lower) 154 (upper)

Dumbarton Oaks,
Trustees for Harvard University
pages 6, 51, 59

Hollehzer Laslo and
Orszagos Muemlek Felugyeloseg
pages 197, 198

Giovanni Marchi
pages 199, 200, 201, 205, (upper) 206, 207

Colour separation and Photosetting by Textype, Artes Gráficas, Lda.
Printed by Snoeck Ducaju & Zoon of Gent, Belgium

Copyright © 1991, M. T. Train / /Scala Books
Photographs © 1991, Nicolas Sapieha
All rights reserved. No part of this book may be reproduced without written permission of the publisher.

Published by
M. T. TRAIN/SCALA BOOKS, NEW YORK

Distributed in the United States and Canada by
RIZZOLI INTERNATIONAL PUBLICATIONS INC.
300 Park Avenue South, New York, NY 10010

Available in the United Kingdom
ANTIQUE COLLECTORS' CLUB

ISBN 0 85667 399 4
LC 91-060288

Opposite page:
A Magnolia soulangeana in
flower by the door decorated with
stucco medallions at Wilanów

GARDENS
IN
CENTRAL EUROPE

Text by Patrick Bowe
Photography by Nicolas Sapieha

EDITED BY PTOLEMY TOMPKINS

M. T. TRAIN / SCALA BOOKS, NEW YORK

Distributed by Rizzoli International Publications Inc.

SWEDEN

DENMARK

USSR

Gdansk

Rostock

Szczecin

ELB

ODRA

WISLA

Berlin

Poznań

POLAND

Warszawa

7

6

GERMANY

2

1

5

Pulawy

7

Leipzig

Dresden

Muskau

5

Wroclaw

3

4

9

Krakow

10

Prague

11

12

13

15

20

14

16

Brno

CZECHOSLOVAKIA

17

18

19

Bratislava

21

23

RUMANIA

22

25

Budapest

Oradea

31

24

HUNGARY

AUSTRIA

Brasov

32

30

Timisoara

34

Llubljana

Zagreb

Bucharest

33

BLACK SEA

Beograd

Craiova

DANUBE

YUGOSLAVIA

BULGARIA

Saravejo

Split

ITALY

29

28

Dubrovnik

27

26

TURKEY

ALBANIA

GREECE

MEDITERRANEAN SEA

CONTENTS

Studnia pod gurą czyli przy Murze.

INTRODUCTION

Central Europe has always formed the gateway between Europe and the Orient. In its gardens, for example, the patterns of Islamic design are overlaid on more conventional European gardening traditions. The first concrete evidence of ornamental gardening in the region, however, lies in the excavated ruins of classical Roman villas. The chain of great villas, including that of Diocletian at Split, which stretch along the Adriatic coast of Yugoslavia, contains terraces, courtyards, formal pools, mosaics and other garden fragments which enable us to reconstruct their gardens' design. Similar remains survive in the excavated towns of Oescus and Nicopolis ad Istrum in Bulgaria.

After the collapse of the Roman Empire, classical gardening traditions were kept alive only in Serbia and Macedonia (now part of southern Yugoslavia) which were then under the influence of the Byzantine Empire. By the more settled eleventh and twelfth centuries, monks from Western Europe were migrating eastwards, building monasteries and creating small cloister gardens of geometric layout filled with vegetables, fruits, herbs, medicinal plants and a scattering of flowers. Such gardens are frequently represented in the background of medieval altars in Hungary and Poland, and in the painted murals on monastery walls in Rumania and Bulgaria. Few original layouts actually survive. However, the Franciscan monastery (1317) in Dubrovnik guards within its cloister an exceptional design of a central path, flanked by rows of stone benches and terminated by a fountain, which is quite different from the usual cross-walk plan.

The peaceable pursuit of gardening was interrupted by the Mongolian invasion (1242) of the eastern part of the region. The later expansion of the Ottoman Empire into the region had a lasting effect on both its architecture and design. In Bulgaria, where Ottoman rule lasted from 1391 to 1878, Islamic gardens were created in the courtyards of many mosques, and in the palaces of the beys and agas. The present City Park of Sofia derives from the garden of the last Turkish *vali*, Makhzar Pasha. In the provinces of Bosnia and Macedonia in southern Yugoslavia, the opulent creativity of the period is still visible in the courtyards of the mosques and in Muslim graveyards, such as the one at Alifakovac near Sarajevo with its elevated position, exquisite tombstones and its original spiral arrangement. The Turks also introduced to Europe many new garden plants. Citrus fruits, pomegranates, many

Study for a fountain at Murze in «Various Thoughts for the Creation of a garden, written by Izabelle Czartoryska, Wroclaw 1808.

7

exotic shrubs, herbs and flowers, particularly tulips in all colours, including green and lilac, are first mentioned in Hungary, during the period of Turkish rule (1541-1686). The areas not under Turkish rule still looked to Western Europe for cultural inspiration. The Italian Renaissance at its height, between the fifteenth and sixteenth centuries, was an overwhelming influence. Before the Turkish invasion of his country, the great Hungarian King Matthias Corvinus (1458-1490) invited Italian scholars and artists to his splendid courts at Buda and Visĕgrad. Ornamental aviaries, fountains, terraces, parterres, even labyrinths, of Renaissance design, as well as many plants imported from Italy, are recorded in the gardens of both palaces. Close ties with North Italy during the height of its humanist culture were maintained by the republic of Dubrovnik (then known as Ragusa). Coastal villas with terraces, pergolas and pools connecting the garden with the sea, followed closely on Italian models. The best preserved of these is the Gothic-Renaissance Sorkocevic Villa at Lapad. Of the dozen or so Renaissance gardens remaining in Poland, those at Baranów, Pieskowa Skala and Brzeg have been recently restored, though the one at Mogilany (circa 1560) with its modest classical layout, its hillside setting and its distant view of the Tatra mountains, is the most evocative.

In the succeeding century, gardens became more elaborate and grandiose in design. The Emperor Rudolph II graced his spectacular court at Prague with a complex of formal gardens richly decorated with statuary and fountains designed by the influential Dutchman, Jan Vredeman de Vries (1527-1606). The nearby Wallenstein Palace of 1626 has an equally sumptuous garden with a *sala terrena* designed by an Italian architect, Giovanni Battista Pironi, and statuary by Adrian de Vries.

A period of great expansion and prosperity began after the defeat of the Turkish army at Vienna in 1688. The popularity of the Baroque style of gardening, developed by the French and epitomized by the royal park at Versailles, spread through Europe reaching Czechoslovakia, Hungary, Poland and Slovenia, the northern part of Yugoslavia which was then part of the Austrian-Hungarian Empire. The style was judiciously adapted to suit the dryer climate of these regions by avoiding the many fountains and other complex water-features which were characteristic of this style of gardening in France. In Hungary more than a hundred such gardens were made but most were subsequently altered or have disappeared. The largest remaining example is Esterháza at Fertöd which, though almost totally destroyed in the last war, has been splendidly restored. Many in Czechoslovakia have likewise disappeared and are only known through engravings. Buchlovice in the Chřiby hills of South Moravia is a beautiful surviving example — its terraces, steps, pools and statues all unchanged and well maintained. Dobříš and Konopiště, both in Central Bohemia, also survive in their original classical French form. Magnificent embroidered parterres, numerous sculptures and clipped trees still decorate the gardens of Nieberow near Lowicz, and at Bialystok and Wilanow near Warsaw in Poland. Although many Baroque layouts were created in Yugoslavia on the Passonian plain between Styria and Vojvodina, the most magnificent is at Dornava near Ptuj in Slovenia. Here a 1.8 km long axis stretches through the house to be terminated by sculpture at either end. An immense, four-part parterre is centred on a fountain figure of Neptune and its rich sculptural programme mostly remains.

The complex formality of such Baroque garden layouts began to seem rigid and anachronistic to the Romantic sensibility which was developing in Europe in the eighteenth century. The more 'naturalistic' effects of the English landscape garden with its extensive, undulating lawns, winding paths and informal sheets of water, better suited the prevailing temperament. In Hungary, a multitude of flowering trees and shrubs were planted in this manner to present charming and informal vistas at Tata, Martonvásár (home of Beethoven's friends, the Brunswick family) and Varosliget, the latter two laid out by the famous German designer, Christian Heinrich Nebbien (1778-1841). In Czechoslovakia, the supreme example of the style is Lednice in South Moravia. Of truly international significance, this park created by the Liechtenstein family, boasts a thirty-four-hectare lake with no less than fifteen islands, a host of romantic park buildings including a minaret (1791) and a curvilinear iron conservatory (1843) by the English architect, G.H. Devien. In Poland, classicist tendencies emerged in conjunction with the landscape style. Temples and rotundas grace the four great parks — Arkadia, Lazienki, Lancut and Pulawy — which are open to the public. Pulawy is of particular interest as it was laid out for Isabela Czartoryska (1746-1835) author of the standard work in Polish on the English landscape garden, *Various Thoughts on the Creation of Gardens* (Wroclaw, 1805 as is in the bibliography).

From the middle of the last century, the growing public interest in botany resulted in the creation of many collections of decorative plants, some eventually becoming arboreta of international significance. Most notable are those of Kórnik and Goluchów in Poland and the famous collection of Count Ambrozy-Migazzi at Malonya, then in Hungary but now in Czechoslovakia. New botanical gardens, like those at Cluj in Transylvania and zoological gardens, like those at Poznań in Poland, were established. Increasing concern with public health and recreation led to the founding of public parks in cities. Park Carol in Bucharest is one of the best examples.

Many of them were laid out on the ruins of the fortifications which had been built to encircle many old towns and cities. The parks in Jindřichův Hradec in Czechoslovakia and Kraków in Poland are of this type. Health concerns were also responsible for the creation of spa resorts like Marienbad and Francenbad which had extensive landscape and flower gardens where the spa's clients would exercise. Bright colour was usually provided by half-hardy or tender annuals just then being imported from South America, South Africa and the tropical areas of the Far East. The floral carpet in front of the great medieval church of Kutná Hora (circa 1380) in Czechoslovakia was an important example of this kind of flower gardening.

As well as these large-scale developments, domestic gardens of smaller, flowering plants were being made. The royal family of Rumania was foremost in introducing these flower gardens to its country. At the Palace of Sinaia, a loggia was wreathed with wisteria; terraces, statuary and parterres were given a delicate clothing of perennial flowering plants. At Potlogi Palace, the vines on an ironwork arcade throw a dappled shade on the walk beneath. At the Cotroceni Monastery near Bucharest, a deliberately archaic arrangement of narrow beds of herbs and flowers was overlooked by a pergola.

In the early part of this century, the modern movement in art and design inspired a series of city villas with architecturally designed gardens of high quality as for example the gardens of Jan Kotěra and Adolf Loos in Prague, the Villa Tugendhat by Mies van der Rohe in Brno and the modifications to the palace gardens in Prague by the Slovenian architect, Josip Plečnik. Current developments include the creation of parks and nature reserves in the environs of the larger towns for public recreation and education. The growth of the mass tourism has resulted in a large-scale landscaping works in the Black Sea resorts of Bulgaria and along the shores of Lake Balaton. Meanwhile, many neglected historical gardens are being reconstructed and restored.

GERMANY
EAST

Germany before the nineteenth century was not so much a unified country as a complex assemblage of separate states. The present boundary that divides Germany and Poland, Saxon and Slav, was established along the Oder river about the year 1000. After this date Germany gradually began to grow into a series of independent city-states. East Germany, which is our concern in this book, stretches from the old Grand Duchy of Mecklenberg along the Baltic Sea to the north, and through the Brandenberg Plain and the former Kingdom of Prussia to the Thuringian Hills and the former Kingdom of Saxony in the south.

Only in the fifteenth century did the powerful dynasty of the Hohenzollerns establish itself in the heart of East Germany at Berlin, thus effectively unifying the whole of Germany. The earliest recorded German garden of any consequence is that built by the Dukes of Weimar in 1448. The Elector of Saxony founded the first botanic garden at Leipzig in 1580. As protection at that time was a prime consideration, the gardens of the Kurfurst in Berlin and Mortizburg in Saxony were surrounded by moats.

The whole of East Germany espoused Protestantism at the Reformation and as a result the country was devastated during the subsequent Thirty Years' War (1618-48). After peace was established, Saxony emerged as the foremost cultural state. Its substantial wealth was based on its extensive deposits of silver ore and its electors acquired great prestige on their election to the Kingdom of Poland during the early eighteenth century. The most important formal Baroque gardens in East Germany, the Grosser Garten (1683) and the Grossedlitz (1719) were laid out near Saxony's capital, Dresden. They both survive though altered, the latter still a place of great, restrained beauty with fountains which play so softly they are known as the 'Stille Musik'. In the neighbouring principality of Anhalt-Dessau, Princess Henrietta Catherine, daughter of the noted dilettante of landscape Prince Frederich Henry of Orange, laid out a Dutch-style formal garden at Oranienbaum in 1683.

Throughout the first half of the eighteenth century, Dresden remained the cultural focus of the region, reaching an apogee in the reign of Augustus III of Saxony (1737-63), when it was known as the German Florence. Artists, craftsmen, musicians and actors flocked to its court where extravagant entertainments were held in the great square known as the

Zwinger. The Zwinger was designed by the architect Matthaeus Daniel Pöppelmann, who also designed a complex of royal summer palaces around the perimeter of the city: at Pillnitz on the Elbe, the Japanese Palace on the outskirts of the city and around the old hunting lodge of Moritzburg. The courtiers also engaged in building and gardening projects. Count Bruhl built his terrace garden with sculpted rivergods overlooking the river in the centre of the city which remains the same today. Ludwig of Wurtemberg-Teck laid out a garden at the Palais Marcolini which still boasts Dresden's finest fountain. Figures represented include Neptune and Amphitrite surrounded by winged seahorses and other fantastic creatures and beneath them figures representing the great rivers of the Tiber and the Nile.

The cultural leadership of Germany passed to Prussia in the middle of the eighteenth century. Prussia's great military commander Frederick the Great had visited Dresden at the height of that city's cultural Renaissance. He began his building and gardening activities at Rheinsberg in Potsdam in 1734. On their completion he handed the palace and sixty-acre park over to his brother and began work on his famous palace and garden of Sans Souci. Sans Souci's most unique feature was the set of seven glazed vine terraces which descended the hill in front of it. Frederick was much criticized in his lifetime for his conservative taste in architecture and gardening. By comparison, the most progressive patron of gardening of the time in Germany was the grandson of his general 'The Old Dessauer', Prince Franz von Anhalt-Dessau (1740-1817), who turned his back on Prussian militarism in favour of the enlightened social, industrial, agricultural, educational and aesthetic reforms taking place in England at the time. His park at Worlitz shows the direct influence of such English parks as Kew, Stowe and Stourhead. His ambitions stretched beyond the creation of individual, private parks to the landscaping of the entire countryside. His pioneering vision of country planning led to the creation of the so-called 'Garden Kingdom', a landscape design of over 150 square miles along the banks of the river Elbe. The 'Garden Kingdom' exerted a most profound influence on Goethe's design of the park at Weimar for his patron, Duke Carl August of Saxe-Weimar. Goethe in turn encouraged Prince Hermann von Puckler-Muskau (1785-1871) to interest himself in landscape gardening. This resulted in the famous park of Muskau, which in its time exerted an important influence on landscaping both in Europe and the United States.

The landscape gardener primarily responsible for the creation of the complex of royal parks around Lake Havel in Potsdam was Peter Joseph Lenné (1789-1866). Lenné was plucked from his position as an assistant gardener by Puckler's father-in-law and Prussia's Chancellor Hardenburg and commissioned to design his park at Klein-Glienicke. In 1833, he was asked to draw up 'A Plan to embellish the Isle of Potsdam' which was another early attempt in country planning. Both Puckler and Lenné had young assistants, Eduard Petzold (1815-1891) and Gustav Meyer (1816-1877) respectively, who were to become East Germany's leading garden designers of the late nineteenth century. Petzold took over the directorship of the park at Muskau after Puckler's departure in 1846 and designed a number of parks in both Holland and Germany. Meyer, who had been in Lenné's drawing office at Sans Souci, became the first director for municipal gardens in the city of Berlin. Thus the tradition of landscape gardening in the English style was handed down in East Germany in an unbroken line from its first exponent to the last.

After Germany's defeat in World War I and the subsequent dissolution of its empire, the introduction of a new order began with a modern, progressive outlook. The impulse for change in gardening and landscape architecture came first from the architectural profession but was soon adopted by a new generation of landscape designers as well. Fritz Encke (1861-1931), who worked in the Berlin Parks Department and taught at the Royal Horticultural School in Potsdam, helped establish the German Society for Garden Art. The society's members called themselves garden architects rather than landscape gardeners in a deliberate attempt to break away from the nineteenth-century tradition of Lenné. Leberecht Migge (1881-1935), who moved to Berlin in 1920, became closely tied with the city's modern architects and designed the gardens for the International Building Exhibition at Leipzig in 1913. Erwin Barth (1880-1933), a pupil of Encke and a friend of Migge, became garden director of Greater Berlin in 1926, later holding the first University Chair of Garden Design in Europe at Berlin's Agricultural University.

Many garden designers of the time who did not attend the Royal Horticultural College or the Agricultural University learned their trade in one of the large horticultural firms such as that of Karl Foerster (1874-1970) in Potsdam or Franz Ludwig Spath in Berlin. Foerster concentrated his efforts as a nurseryman and designer on the use of modern perennials, employing such talented plantsmen as Camillo Schneider and Hermann Mattern (1902-1971) whereas Spath, interested in woody plants, nurtured the talents of Otto Valentien (b. 1897), his chief designer from the 1920s. Mattern, who also worked briefly with Migge, was one of the most influential figures in post-war German garden design, becoming Professor of Garden and Landscape Design at Berlin University in 1961. Both Mattern and Valentien softened the severe architectural styles of the early part of the century with a rich varied peren-

nial planting. Under their influence gardens became less architectural and more concentrated on planting design, thus paving the way for the German pioneers of the movement for the ecological use of native plants which has been characteristic of German gardens since the end of World War II.

SANS SOUCI

The growing of table grapes in greenhouses is widespread in north Central Europe, but the cultivation in sufficient numbers to make a table wine is practically unknown with the exception of the glazed vineyard made by Frederick the Great (1712-1786) at Potsdam in 1744. The hillside chosen by Frederick overlooked the River Havel near the elaborate kitchen garden made by his father (known sarcastically as the Marlygarten after Louis XIV's pleasure pavilion at Versailles).

Frederick had six terraces cut into the south-facing slope and subsequently glazed each to protect the vines growing on the retaining wall. To maximize light and heat, each terrace was in the form of a shallow parabolic curve.

In 1745 after the vineyard had come into production, Frederick sketched out a plan for a small summer palace to stand above this apparent cascade of glass. He asked his architect, George Woncesinus von Knobelsdorff (1699-1753) to develop

his sketch into a practical design for a bachelor palace. Frederick was already living apart from his wife, but he needed another place where he and a small circle of friends might on occasion escape from the cares of royal life: the palace was later entitled 'Sans Souci' literally 'without care'. The need to escape the stiff ceremonial of court had been well established among monarchs since Louis XIV built the Trianon in the park at Versailles. The rooms at Sans Souci were small and intimate, exquisitely decorated and of complicated shape and arrangement. Their *ambiance* was designed to promote the intimate social arts of conversation, letter-writing, chamber music, dancing, manners and seduction. The principal reception rooms were not on the first floor as in a great palace, but on the ground floor, where each could have direct access to the garden through the newly invented 'french' window. Frederick and his architect, von Knobelsdorff, were old friends. When Frederick's father had entrusted him with his first position of responsibility as colonel of the regiment near Ruppin, von Knobelsdorff was one of his fellow officers. Frederick had him design a little garden temple dedicated to Almathea which is extant. The Protestant von Knobelsdorff was very suspicious of Italian architecture, preferring Greek-inspired colonnades, vases and statues. As a result his design for the entrance court, entrance façade and entrance hall of Sans Souci, is determinedly neo-Classical. Outside, similarly conservative choices were made. Frederick insisted on retaining his own preferred Rococo style on the garden front. Rather than pairs of pilasters such as those which divide the windows at the Grand Trianon at Versailles, Frederick preferred to have pairs of 'terms', or sculpted figures on pedestals, between the windows at Sans Souci. Terms are usually designed to hold a heavy lintol but here they play a merely decorative role; the figures appear to hang from the parapet and twine garlands of roses and vines — the latter an appropriate decorative motif for a palace in a vineyard. They may have been inspired by the similarly light-hearted terms created by Permosa for the Zwinger Palace in Dresden, which Frederick visited as a boy. The union of architecture and sculpture, typical of the Rococo style, failed to impress the Prince de Ligne, Belgian garden expert, on his visit in 1770. He thought it outmoded, provincial and overdone in comparison with the severe, classical style then in vogue at Versailles. Frederick and von Knobelsdorff disagreed on a number of points concerning Sans-Souci's design. The architect wanted the building raised above a cellar level to avoid the rising damp,

Sans Souci

An equestrian figure of King Frederick William IV is silhouetted in front of an enormous orangery designed by Persius c. 1850.

*Opposite page:
The curving steps of the rococo picture gallery designed by J.C. Buring in 1763, descend into the garden.*

Sans Souci
*The entrance court designed by
G.W. Knobelsdorff is enclosed by
a curving colonnade of
Corinthian columns which are
repeated on the entrance façade
and in the entrance hall to give a
rare exterior and interior
architectural unit.*

Top:
*The art of trelliswork reached a
peak of sophistication in the
eighteenth century. Arcades of
trellis cast a dappled shade across
the palace terraces.*

*Rhododendrons flower across the
moat from the palace. The
sphinxes in the background are by
Eberhech.*

and situated near the edge of its terrace so that it could be seen in its entirety from the garden below. Frederick refused to capitulate in both cases, and the results were just as von Knobelsdorff feared. The palace is only partially visible from the terraces beneath it, and has consistently been judged to be seriously defective in its design. Frederick was at his happiest at Sans Souci. Among the diversions he organized were concerts, in which he played the flute, and *fêtes galantes* — the informal but elegant garden parties often depicted by Watteau, whose works Frederick collected for the palace. Here he received such luminaries as Voltaire, who first visited in July of 1750. In the intervals between his military campaigns, Frederick customarily returned to Sans Souci to play with his 'dolls' — as he called his art collections — and to keep abreast of the many buildings and gardening projects that were always under way.

Frederick was fond of having fresh-fruit on his table year round. A number of speculators built glasshouses in Berlin to keep him supplied, but he later started a fruit garden of his own at Sans Souci which included melons grown from seed imported from Italy. Aside from the cultivation of fruit, his interest in gardening seems to have been limited by an apparently unsuccessful attempt to reconcile the classical horticultural techniques described in Virgil's *Georgics* with those of contemporary German practice. Prince de Ligne once opined of Virgil: 'A great poet, Sire, but what a bad gardener'.

Sans Souci
The Chinese Tea House (1754-57) was designed by J.G. Buring after a sketch by Frederick the Great. The roof is supported on gilded columns simulating palm trees.

A lifesize, gilded figure plays the mandolin between the verandah columns.

'To whom do you say it', replied the king. 'Have I not tried to plant, hoe, dig and sow with the *Georgics* in my hand. My man says to me 'Monsier, you are a fool and so is your book — that's not the way to work'. On another occasion Frederick wrote to his Scottish friend, Lord Keith: 'I read Virgil's *Georgics* in the morning. I send my gardener to the devil for he says neither Virgil nor I know anything about gardening.' He frequently employed gardening metaphors in his discussions of people and nations. Of man's predestined fate on earth he explained, 'God, like a gardener, sows people as they are —narcissus, jasmine, marigold, carnation and violet — and leaves them all to grow without interference here on earth.' Italy he likened to an ancient garden gone to seed which, since all the alleys, vases and statues still existed, could easily be fertilized to flower again.

The intimacy of Sans Souci's Rococo style has been assured by buildings individually designed for each separate function. The main palace is flanked by freestanding trellis pavilions and by further pavilions housing the guest quarters and the art gallery designed by Johann Gottfried Buring in 1760. The intimacy of the garden design is conserved by separate hedged enclosures or outdoor 'rooms'. A note of levity is added by the use of children rather than the usual solemn deities as models for the sculpture in the garden of the gallery.

The main vista from the palace retains an informal atmosphere terminating in gardeners' cottages rather than in an architectural monument.

Despite Sans Souci's overall informality, Frederick did have a conventional parterre laid out below the vineyard. At the centre was a fountain depicting the story of the sea-nymph Thetis, a favourite subject for Rococo garden sculpture. It was surrounded by Air and Water figures sculpted by J.S. Adam and figures of Mercury and Venus sculpted by Pigalle and presented to Frederick by Louis XV. The remainder of the park featured important sculpture by Glune such as the Rondel of the Muses and the Rondel of the Rape. Glune also provided a Bacchus and Ariadne group, and Eberhech a famous pair of sphinxes.

Frederick was continually adding new 'toys' to his park. Von Knobelsdorff designed the Obelisk Portal in 1747, and the Neptune Grotto and the Marble Colonnade in 1751. At the end of the Seven Years' War Frederick, though close to financial ruin, undertook the building of a large summer palace, the Neues Palais, to house his court and state visitors. As von Knobelsdorff had since died, it was designed by Buring, Manger and Gonthard. Gonthard alone designed the later Temple of Friendship and Temple of Antiquity located nearby.

Sans Souci

Detail from the Chinese Tea House. More lifelike wooden figures, in a marriage of oriental subject and western sculptural style.

Frederick the Great was an accomplished flautist and a composer. Hence the appropriateness of the musical instruments used as decorations on the trelliswork.

Of all Frederick's follies at Sans Souci, none has excited imaginations more than the Chinese Tea House (1754-56). Executed by Buring after a sketch by the king, its furniture, porcelains and silks are covered with motifs from the Far East. Fanciful visions of the Orient had been introduced to Prussia by Frederick's grandfather, and Frederick himself corresponded with Voltaire on the intricacies of the philosophy of Confucius. Trefoil in plan, the tea house has a conical roof supported by columns in simulation of gilded palm trees. Casually spaced between the columns are groups of life-size figures; one group is in the midst of a tea ceremony while a group of girls is being enticed by offerings of pineapples and mangoes. In another stroke of fantasy, a Mandarin perches under a parasol on the roof apex. Such figures attracted the scorn of at least one contemporary, who wrote, 'We know, at any rate, that the Chinese though they put...images of their gods inside the temples, did not put them on their roofs. Still less did they place figures of themselves drinking tea or smoking tobacco...in front of their buildings.'

Sans Souci now stands in a landscape created in the early nineteenth century during the reign of Frederick William IV. Like his ancestor, Frederick William was an amateur architect and patron of the leading architects of the day. He commissioned Peter Joseph Lenné to make a comprehensive redesign of the park in a romantic English style. Karl Friedrich Schinkel, the great Prussian architect, often regarded as the forerunner of Modernism, was commissioned to collaborate on the architectural work. After Schinkel's death in 1841 the role was taken by his pupil Persius. The buildings which adorned the newly recreated park were in an informal style based on fifteenth-and sixteenth-century Italian farmhouses. Not only were the residences of the king and the court designed in this style but also the houses of the estate staff such as gardeners, boatmen and water engineers. Functional buildings such as water towers and the steam turbine house were not hidden away but given prominence by being designed in the same style. Later, a typical nineteenth-century eclecticism crept into the design of the new park buildings: a lakeside church was built in an Early Christian basilica style, and a new building for the estate waterworks was modelled on an Egyptian mosque. Despite these extensive changes, Frederick the Great's little palace of Sans Souci remains the focal point of the park.

Potsdam is one of the few areas on the flat, sandy plain of Brandenburg with an abundance of wood and water. The Havel river and its adjacent canal widen occasionally to give the appearance of a chain of extensive lakes around the town. A whole complex of summer residences and parks grew up along its banks but its unity has been impaired until recently by the paraphernalia of the political frontier which divided it. With German political unity restored, it may yet be possibile to return much of this wonderful landscape to its former glory.

WORLITZ

The Temple of Venus built in 1794 in imitation of the same temple by Colin Campbell at Hall Barn, England.

Worlitz, one of the first landscape parks in Continental Europe, was begun in 1765, the year after its owner, Prince Franz von Anhalt-Dessau (1740-1817), made his first visit to England. It had a decisive influence on subsequent landscape parks in Germany, in particular the park at Weimar made by the Duke Carl August of Weimar and his friend the great writer Johann Wolfgang Goethe, who first visited Worlitz in 1778. The Duke admired Worlitz so much that he later presented the park with one of its ornamental buildings, an Italian-style farmhouse.

Prince von Anhalt-Dessau's concept of landscaping went far beyond the creation of an individual private park. He proposed that the entire countryside, including the town and the agricultural and forestry lands, should be planned and planted with an eye to beauty. The prince went on to demonstrate his theory in practice by developing his *Gartenreich* or 'Garden Kingdom', which covered an area of about fifty-five square miles and stretched for over fifteen miles along the banks of the river Elbe. A series of parks — Schloss Dessau, Oranienbaum, Mosigkau, Worlitz, Luisium, Sieglitzer Berg, Georgium and Grosskuhnau — were designed as self-contained units also connected by carefully planned areas of countryside which continued to be put to agricultural use. This broadened concept of landscaping influenced the subsequent creation of the complex of royal parks around the city of

Worlitz

The South Sea Pavilion built in 1783 in recognition of the fact that many of Prince von Anhalt-Dessau's English role-models had derived their wealth from the South Sea Company.

Potsdam outside Berlin. The concept was also taken up by Prince Hermann Puckler in developing his estate at Muskau. From here it spread to the United States where the elevated status of country planning eventually resulted in the development of the American metropolitan park system.

As a young man, von Anhalt-Dessau had reacted against growing Prussian militarism in favour of the progressive agricultural, industrial and social reforms of liberal England. These he tried to introduce in his own principality of Dessau. His second source of inspiration was the enlightened individualist philosophy of the French writer Jean-Jacques Rousseau, to whom he dedicated a poplar-planted island in the lake at Worlitz in 1782. Rousseau's influence on the park-makers of the time is evidenced by the dedication to him of similar islands in other parks as far afield as Tiefurt near Berlin, Arkadia in Poland and the more famous contemporaneous French park, Ermenonville, near Paris. Von Anhalt-Dessau's third source of inspiration was Johann Joachim Winckelmann (1717-1768), the German classical archaeologist and historian. Winckelmann revived interest in ancient art and was one of the founders of neo-Classicism which influenced the style of many of the buildings in Worlitz's park.

Von Anhalt-Dessau's role-models, however, were the great Whig or Liberal aristocrats of England whose parks at Stowe,

The Gothic House (1773), the first neo-Gothic garden building in continental Europe based on a model of Shotover Park, Oxfordshire.

26

The Synagogue built in 1790 was based on Peruzzi's circular churches at Celsa and San Galgano, Italy.

Stourhead and Claremont functioned as centres of enlightenment that helped provide a strong counterweight to the conservative royal court. In 1767, together with the architect von Erdmansdorff, with whom he was to work for the next thirty years, he began to build a new house, its design based on an English model published in James Gibbs *A Book of Architecture* (1728). Being the first neo-Classical-style house in Central Europe, its subsequent influence was enormous. Three years later disaster struck, when the entire park around the house was flooded. Flooding has always been a problem in Central Europe where many of the rivers are fed by snowmelt from high mountains. The flood-control system which von Anhalt-Dessau had taken the precaution of installing turned out to be ineffective. However, disaster was turned to advantage by transforming the flooded area into a permanent lake known as the Kleines Walloch. Around this the architect began to create a new area of parkland called Schoch's Garden after his landscape gardener, Johann Georg Schoch (1758-1826). In this garden in subsequent years he built a series of outstanding park buildings based on English models. The neo-Gothic style of architecture was introduced to continental Europe in 1773 with a Gothic house based on a structure at Shotover Park, Oxfordshire. The White Bridge built over a nearby canal in the same year, was based on

The Nymphaeum was created in 1767-68 by erecting a classical portico in front of a former underground ice house.

Worlitz

The Rousseau Island created in 1782 as a symbol of the prince's sympathy with Rousseau's liberal philosophy.

The narrow peep over the classical bridge to the synagogue behind has been enhanced by pruning of the overhanging trees letting the light in on the water. Another peep leads the eye leftwards to the tower of the neo-Gothic parish church built in 1805.

Sir William Chamber's Chinese Bridge in Kew Gardens, London. The Temple of Venus, built in 1774, matches the English architect Colin Campbell's Temple at Hall Barn in Buckinghamshire. A memorial urn erected to von Anhalt-Dessau's uncle and mentor, Prince Dietrich, the following year was based on an urn erected by the poet Alexander Pope in his garden at Twickenham in the Thames. By 1780, he was also designing *faux-naif* or deliberately 'primitive' areas in the park in premeditated reference to prehistoric man. These were decorated with glacial erratics and other oddly shaped boulders and given names such as the Skaldic Graves. The num-

ber of new constructions peaked in 1781; von Anhalt-Dessau began work on a romantic area with artificial 'ruins', a hermit's cave, a chain-bridge, cliffs, grottoes and rock formations — all of which predate the similar but better known constructions in the park of Mereville in France. A South Sea Pavilion was built in recognition of the fact that many of the prince's English role-models had derived their wealth from the South Sea Company, but in the midst of all this activity the park was again flooded. An eternal optimist von Anhalt-Dessau again turned the flooded area into a new permanent lake. This one he called the Grosses Walloch, and around it

he created another new area of parkland during the 1790s known as the New Plantation. These new lands were characterized by a much broader sweep of landscape and planting than the earlier areas. On one of the access canals an allegorical set of buildings called the Stein was erected featuring a great mound of stones representing Vesuvius. On occasion a bonfire was lit in the 'volcano' to represent an eruption. On its slope he built an Italian-style cottage called the Villa Hamilton in honour of the British archaeologist Sir William Hamilton who had promoted the excavation that brought the ancient city of Pompeii to light. Elsewhere in the New

Worlitz
The White Bridge built in 1773
in imitation of Sir Chamber's
Chinese bridge at Kew, near
London. Note its clear span
without intermediate support.

Aesculus x carnea — *smaller in*
stature and later in flower than
the common horse chestnut.

Plantation von Anhalt-Dessau's new building followed English models. In 1791 he constructed an iron bridge, a replica of the most modern bridge of the time erected twenty years earlier at Coalbrookdale in Shropshire. In 1795 he built the Pantheon, in imitation of the building in the park at Stourhead, Wiltshire, to house his collection of Antique sculpture. During the 1790s he also continued to erect ornamental buildings in the older part of the park. Stourhead was again the model for the Temple of Flora erected in the flower garden in 1797.

The park structures listed above do not exhaust the catalogue of ornamental buildings constructed by von Anhalt-Dessau during the forty-two years he spent developing Worlitz. There are commemorative monuments, stone tablets with bas-relief sculpture or inscriptions, one, warning against the maltreatment of the natural world, is of acute contemporary relevance,

a Jewish synagogue and cemetery, a Gothic-style school stables and a parish church.

During the same period, the prince was either restoring or recreating no fewer than seven other houses and their parks. In each of these he erected park buildings often based on English models. The pagoda at Oranienbaum and the Ruined Arch at Dessau are both after Sir William Chamber's originals at Kew. The orangery at Oranienbaum, erected in 1812, had some 300 orange trees and was considered to be the finest in Europe of it time. Although Goethe wrote satirically of the large number of garden buildings erected by the prince, he nevertheless valued the Gartenreich's Elysian mood. Today the prodigious number of structures is less obvious as the trees of the park have grown to mask or screen many from immediate view. Certainly there is no gainsaying Prince Franz von Anhalt-Dessau's achievement in creating what is among the first of the great landscape parks of Europe.

WEIMAR-BELVEDERE

The rooftop terrace and summerhouse gave the palace its name of Belvedere. Part of the formal baroque garden designed with the house by J.A. Richter c. 1725, was retained when the park was relandscaped in 1850. The hedge-enclosed garden rooms have clipped limes for height among the gravel walks and box-edged flowerbeds in carefully controlled colour schemes.

Situated on the banks of the river Ilm among the forested Thuringian Hills, Weimar is closely associated with the German literary world of the early nineteenth century. It was during this period that the writers Schiller, Goethe and Herder all lived there under the patronage of Duchess Anna Amalia of Saxe-Weimar and her son Duke Carl August.

The early garden history of Weimar begins in 1448 at a time when the Saxe-Weimar family was consolidating its hold on the region. They laid out a twelve-compartment garden to the south of the castle. The family built a summer palace in the Eishenleite Hills to the south of the town in 1727. Known as the Belvedere, it was designed by the architect J.A. Richter, who in 1739 designed the horseshoe-shaped orangery as well. In 1756 Richter completed a plan for Weimar in the traditional star-shape of a hunting park — the various sections containing the game enclosures. In 1766 the Duchess Anna Amalia extended the park before handing it over to her son in 1780. She then began work on a new garden at Tiefurt, south of the city where she hosted literary evenings attended by Schiller and Goethe and erected such structures as a Temple to the Muses and memorials to Mozart, Herder, Virgil, Duke Leopold of Braunschweig and Schiller among others.

Johann Wolfgang von Goethe (1744-1832) was the principal influence on the parks at Weimar. The notoriously eclectic Sage of Weimar counted landscape design among his many interests. Goethe's involvement with the art of garden planning is made manifest in such books as *Elective Affinities* (1769), and through the plans he devised for his own garden at Weimar and for the ducal park around it, and in his contribution to the plant collections at Belvedere Palace. Goethe's interest in landscaping was said to have been awakened by his visit to the park at Worlitz in 1778 and by the writings of the Danish professor C.C.L. Hirschfeld (1742-1792). Hirschfeld maintained in his *The Theory of Garden Art* (1779-81) that garden art should awaken the feelings of sorrow, happiness or surprise with variety in planting and by the use of sentimental inscriptions on monuments or ornamental buildings. Goethe was invited to live at Weimar by Duke Carl August in 1775. The following year he bought himself a summer house in the ducal park around which he laid out a one-acre garden. A picturesque rockface across the river from his house prompted him to commence a little landscaping work in the park outside his garden. In 1778, to gain access to the rockface he built a simple bridge known as the Natural Bridge. Cutting steps in the rockface, he eventually made a grotto with an extremely narrow entrance known as the Eye of the Needle. A thatched wooden hut with adjoining artificial ruins gave further evidence of the eighteenth century's pervasive fascination with nature and the primitive. Here Duke Carl August retired on occasion from the tedious sophistication of palace life, later extending the hut and roofing it with rough shingle so that it came to be known as the Bark House. In due course the duke abandoned the Bark House in favour of a structure known as the Roman House. Built under

Belvedere — Goethe's House
A simple, neo-classical gateway in trelliswork marks the entry to the garden.

Goethe's influence as a neo-Classical Ionic temple, this structure had the benefit of being situated so that it could be seen from many parts of the park.

In 1780 Duke Carl August began to relandscape the park of his summer palace at Belvedere, developing it as a park of botanical as well as landscape significance. Both Goethe and the duke studied botany under the garden director Johann Conrad Sckell (1768-1834), a member of an old Thuringian family that had been active in gardening since the seventeenth century. The old orangery was extended to accomodate the new collections, which numbered among their contributors Baron von Humboldt (1769-1859), the most famous German naturalist of his time. The list of rare plants was published and illustrated in the *Catalogus Belvedereanus* in 1820. After his death, Sckell was succeeded as director of the garden by his brother, Johann Christian (1733-1857).

In 1844 the parks of Ilm and Tiefurt were given new life under the direction of Eduard Petzold (1815-1891), a landscape gardener who had come under the influence of the great amateur landscape gardener Prince Hermann von Puckler-Muskau. Petzold was able to use the rapidly maturing trees along the Ilm to create highly picturesque new riverside scenery. At Tiefurt, he extended the existing park so that it too followed more closely the line of the river. The Saxe-Weimar family owned the parks until 1918; since the 1970s all three have been under restoration.

PILLNITZ

From 1718 to 1945, Pillnitz, with its palace and fifty-seven acre garden on a sheltered reach of the river Elbe, was the summer residence of the rulers of Saxony. Pillnitz is located in the heart of 'Saxon Switzerland' an area characterized by extraordinary natural rock forms caused by long-term erosion of the riverside cliffs made famous through the paintings of Caspar David Friedrich (1774-1840), the most romantic of Germany's landscape painters who lived in nearby Dresden. Augustus the Strong, King of Poland and Elector of Saxony, owner of Pillnitz, and his architect, Matthaeus Daniel Pöppelmann (1662-1736), had just completed the famous arena for court entertainments known as the Zwinger in Dresden when they embarked on their second project together, the recreation of the summer palace at Pillnitz. In 1718, Pöppelmann designed the Water Palace, an imposing structure connected to the bank of the river by a monumental, curving, sphinx-guarded flight of steps which was echoed later in many of Friedrich's paintings. In 1723 Pöppelmann designed a matching building known as the Hill Palace at the base of a hill some 150 yards away and connected the two with an immense formal parterre garden of four pools and twelve compartments. To one side he made a suite of hornbeam-hedged 'outdoor rooms' known as the Charmillen. These were designed to house a variety of court entertainments such as

37

a shooting range, skittles and bowling alleys, a grotto, water-jokes and trick-fountains. On the other side of the parterre a long straight avenue of chestnuts led to Dresden. The two palaces which resembled each other so closely they looked like mirror images, were known at the time as the Indian Pavilions, a vague reference, typical of the time, to the somewhat oriental appearance of their roof and their painted Chinese frieze. A similar lack of precision characterized the name given to Pöppelmann's Japanese Palace (1725-35) near Dresden: the name was an expression not of the architectural style as one might expect but of the contents; it was built to house Augustus the Strong's collection of Japanese porcelain. In 1778 the garden was extended during the creation of a new landscape garden containing a small lake with an island on which stood a bronze copy of the second century B.C. sculpture, Juno Ludovisi. The original figure, now in the Capitoline Museum in Rome, was praised by Michelangelo as 'the most beautiful object in the whole of Rome'. Its realistic sculptured drapery was admired by many German writers through the years, including Goethe, who described it in his *Italian Journeys*.

In 1784 an English Pavilion with characteristically plain architecture was designed for the garden by Christian Friedrich Schuricht, who was to be involved in work on the

Pillnitz
The 1718 roofline pagoda-like cupolas and chimneys were matched in the post-1867 restoration of the garden with informal rhododendron hedges.

estate for the next forty-two years. In 1785 he built a neo-Gothic ruin as a focal point in the outer park, in 1804 a Chinese pavilion based on the English architect Sir William Chamber's book, *Designs of Chinese Buildings* (1757), and most important of all, between 1818 and 1826, the New Palace, which linked Pöppelmann's two pavilions. By 1867 the garden had become dilapidated, but a new era in its development began with the appointment of the designer Carl F. Bouche (1850-1933). Bouche restored the garden between the two pavilions to its present design of regularly-shaped grass plots around a central pool. Red gravel paths contrast effectively with the green of the grass and the surrounding wall of forest trees which is broken only by a pair of gigantic copper beeches where the horse chestnut lined avenue begins. Bouche also created an orangery in front of which he laid out a flower garden with a figure of Flora sculpted by Wilf von Hayer in 1870. In spring the beds are filled with bright red tulips edged with white petunia, all seen against the flowering of hardy rhododendron hybrids in the surrounding shrubbery. In 1874 Bouche made a pinetum with over 200 cultivars, many of which have reached outstanding size today. A nearby *Camellia japonica* was planted in the open in 1860 and is protected each winter by a heated greenhouse temporarily put in position over it. Bouche's last work was the creation of the Lilac Garden next to the New Palace. This garden is composed primarily of Rouen or Chinese lilac shrubs, *Syringa x chinensis* — the latter a misnomer since the plant originated in cultivation in the Rouen Botanic Garden around 1777 and does not occur in China at all. Its further hybridization became a passion in France in the nineteenth century, many new forms being marketed by the nursery firms of Emile Lemoine and Messrs Simon-Louis, some of which are represented here. The American landscape architect Charles Eliot visited by boat from Dresden in 1886, his notes evoke the place:

Pillnitz
The formal garden was restored in 1867 by Carl F. Bouche. A pair of purple beech marks the entrance avenue leading to Dresden.

Opposite page:
The sphinx-guarded flight of steps designed by Pöppelmann reaches the river Elbe.

«Took a steamer from the quay below Bruhl Terrace up river....winding river, often high-banked, to the waterside schloss of Pillnitz, a part of the grounds pseudo-Japanese enclosing a formal Renaissance garden with old oranges in tubs, high hedges of the labyrinth variety, and a good avenue of Horse Chestnuts. Between the foot of the high hills is an arboretum, moderately old, most of the modern introductions. After lunch charming views over river meadows to the distant blue hills and the fantastic rock-forms of the foot-hills of the 'Saxon Switzerland'.»

MUSKAU-BRANITZ

Muskau
The neo-Renaissance castle erected in 1863 was gutted in the last days of World War II but its ruins have been conserved to act as a focal point in the park.

An artificial watercourse was dug to drain the marshland around the castle and to feed a newly-made lake.

Between Cottbus and Lubben near the Polish frontier, the river Spree, which has its source in the mountains of Lausitz, divides into hundreds of tributaries. This tranquil series of waterways, where even today punts ply in the shade of overhanging beech trees, is the setting for one of East Germany's most admired gardens. Prince Hermann von Puckler-Muskau (1785-1871), who inherited the estate of Muskau, took an early interest in landscape architecture. He visited Goethe at Weimar in 1812, who advised him to pursue his interest: 'Follow this direction. You seem to have a flair for it. The study of nature is most rewarding if also the most unfathomable — it makes those happy who want to be.' In 1816 he made his first journey to England to study its parks and came under the influence of Humphrey Repton, then the principal exponent of the landscape style in England, whose books were influential in spreading the style on the continent.

On his return, Puckler commissioned the painter August Wilhelm Schirmer (1802-1866) to sketch ideal parkland views including two bodies of water. These drawings were then used as guides for the relandscaping of the park. The marshland was drained to create meadows along the bank of the Neisse

river bisecting Muskau's domain. In the process he created an artificial watercourse to feed a new lake which he had dug around the house. This lake was drained over a series of romantic, rocky waterfalls in 1824 to create a second body of water known as the Oak Lake because of its oak-leafed shape. The soil dug out of the lakes was redistributed to form artificial mounds by a workforce of some 200 men under the direction of Puckler's head gardener, Heinrich Rehder (1790-1852). In 1817 Puckler married an heiress who enabled him to further extend his plans. Sixteen bridges and viaducts were built to connect the park's various parts. Ramps with gilded lions by the Berlin sculptor E. Wolff led down from the castle into an extensive pleasure ground and into the Blue Garden and the Master's Garden beyond. Huge beech, oak and lime, already some 100 years old gave the park an already mature appearance. The great Prussian architect Karl Friedrich Schinkel was commissioned to remodel the castle but Puckler was ultimately unable to afford to put the proposal into effect. He did manage, however, to build a small retreat in the park known as the English House in 1820. No sooner had Puckler completed his landscaping work than he began

Muskau
A magificent free-standing specimen of purple beech by the castle ramp.

to suffer doubts about his efforts, thinking them 'too stiff and derivative', In 1821 he wrote to his admired mentor Humphrey Repton, to seek his advice, A reply arrived from his son John Adey Repton, informing him that his father had died but that he himself would be happy to travel to Muskau and advise. Repton stayed four weeks and succeeded in giving Puckler renewed confidence in his projects.

Puckler travelled to England in 1826 and again in 1829 where he found new inspiration, publishing an account of his last visit. Two years later he published his widely-read *Hints on Landscape Gardening* and went travelling in North Africa and the Near East. In 1843 he was invited to Potsdam to complete the landscaping of the park at Babelsberg for the future Emperor Wilhelm I.

Puckler's landscaping concept was an extravagant one. For example, he advocated creating large areas of parkland with

no thought for profitable or agricultural use despite the fact that he himself had inherited an estate encumbered with debt. His financial situation became such that in 1846, at the age of sixty, he decided to sell Muskau to Prince Frederick of the Netherlands. Prince Frederick's intention was to complete the park as Puckler had intended, taking his advice on the appointment of a garden director who would carry out the task. Puckler recommended Eduard Petzold (1815-1891) with whom he had collaborated on the parks at Ettersburg and

Weimar. Petzold remained at Muskau for almost thirty years, extending the parkland into the hills opposite the castle until it reached a size of over 1,700 acres. In 1875 he made a famous arboretum of over 3,000 cultivars including the largest collection of rare oak forms then to be seen in Europe. This collection was neglected at the end of the century and is now but a common woodland. Fortunately, Petzold's catalogue, *Arboretum Muskaviense* (1864), survives to confirm its former riches.

Petzold executed landscaping schemes on other estates, the most notable of which were at Altobern near Cottbus and at Greiz near Gera. Later he landscaped parks at The Hague and at Twickel in the Netherlands for Prince Frederick. He wrote a number of books, among them *A Contribution on Landscape Gardening* (1849), *Landscape Gardening* (1867) and *A Memoir of my Work* (1890).

Meanwhile, Prince van Puckler-Muskau had retired to a nearby family estate at Branitz. Here he had a canvas of just 200 acres to work with — a considerable step down from 1,700 acres at Muskau. Nonetheless, he set about its landscaping with renewed vigour. The house and its immediate surroundings were altered to the designs of Germany's principal architectural theoretician of the time, Gottfried Semper. The two farmhouses were given ornamental neo-Gothic façades and connected by a pergola, also designed by Semper, which

was decorated with statues by the Danish sculptor Albert Bertel Thorwaldsen. Starting in 1850, he put in place in rapid succession the Pleasure Ground enclosed by a gilded railing, the Blue Garden, the Smithy Garden, the Rose Mount, the Moon Mount, the Island of Venus and a Kiosk with a bust of the singer Henriette Soontag. The park director Georg Blayer created two new lakes, the Pyramid Lake and the Serpentine Lake. In the first was erected a pyramid (1854-56) to contain the burial chamber of the prince and his wife on which was engraved this inscription from the Koran: 'Graves are the mountain tops of a distant, lovely land'. Two further pyramids were erected, the Stepped Pyramid (1863) and the unfinished Hermann's Mount.

Puckler's influence on the world of landscape gardening was immense, Charles Eliot (1859-1997), the Boston-based landscape architect who was a pupil and later partner of Frederick Law Olmsted, noted about Muskau on his trip to Europe in 1886: 'Altogether it is the most remarkable and lovable park I have seen on the Continent...this work of Prince von Puckler-Muskau is of a sort to make me proud of my profession'. Henry Vincent Hubbard (1875-1947) included illustrations of the park in his *An Introduction to the Study of Landscape Design* (1919), a standard text for many years. The park also served as a first-hand inspiration to Adolph Strauss, a pioneer of landscape architecture in the United States and Alfred Rehder, the eminent dendrologist from the Arnold Arboretum in Boston. Both worked at Muskau in their youth.

The park was divided after World War II when the Neisse river was made the new boundary between Germany and Poland. Today approximately 850 of the park's 1,350 acres are in Poland, the remainder in Germany. The park's architecture was also affected by the war, the neo-Renaissance castle built by Prince Frederick of the Netherlands in 1863 to replace Puckler Muskau's house was gutted in the last days of the conflict and the Funeral Church built opposite the castle in 1887 was also demolished. Yet interest in the prince and his work remains vital. A biography entitled *A Prince and his Garden* was published in 1981 by the last private owner of Muskau, Hermann Graf von Arnim. Prince von Puckler-Muskau's own writings have recently been republished and there is a flourishing Puckler Society in Germany.

Branitz
A light iron arbour, in imitation of an Ottoman kiosk, was constructed to shelter a bust of singer Henriette Soontag.

Opposite page:
In 1854, the Earth Pyrami was raised in the centre of an artificial lake as a burial mound for the prince and his wife.

POLAND

Poland is a country of vast sandy plains, forests and low-lying marshes which extends from the Baltic Sea in the north as far as the Carpathian mountains in the south. No similar natural barriers guard its frontiers to the east and west, and as a result the country has constantly expanded and contracted in size throughout its history. It is frequently claimed that only the inner triangle of land between Poźnan, Warsaw and Cracow is 'truly' Polish. The country's continental climate is severe, cold in winter and hot and dry in summer. The soils, with the exception of the fertile brown clays of Silesia, are sandy and poor.

The name 'Poland' meaning 'field' or 'plain', does not appear until the tenth century when the Slavic tribes, long settled in the area, began to organize themselves into a single political unit. In the year 1000 Benedictine monks, followed in 1145 by Cistercians, came from France and set up abbeys with orchards and gardens of vegetables and medicinal herbs. Orchards of 500 apple and pear trees are frequently mentioned. Castles such as Bolkow (c.1300) and Chojuk (1369) are also recorded as having gardens. Urban gardens existed at this time in addition to those of the rural monasteries and castles. The twelfth-century Arabian geographer Al-Idrisi describes Cracow as 'a beautiful large city, with many houses and inhabitants, marketplaces, vineyards and gardens'.

King Sigismund I, who reigned from 1506 to 1548, played a large part in bringing the Italian Renaissance to Poland, especially after his second marriage to Bona Sforza of Milano in 1518. Italian architects such as Santi Gucci designed new houses and laid out formal, axial and symmetrical gardens around them. These include Baranów, one of the best preserved Renaissance houses in Central Europe, and Ksiaz, whose gardens and pavilions dating from the period are now neglected. Sigismund I was succeeded by Sigismund II who saw Poland rise to the peak of its power and prosperity as a result of the Polish-Lithuanian Commonwealth in 1569. Stretching from the Baltic to the Black Sea, it comprised the largest political unit in Europe at the time. The classical layout of the garden at Mogilany with its distant view of the Tatra mountains, and the pavilions and terraced gardens at Mirov near Cracow both date from this period. Sigismund II had no heirs, as a result of which he established 'the democracy of the nobles' whereby each successive king would be elected by an assembly of the nobles. The first king so

elected was Sigismund III, who also served as King of Sweden. Sigismund III moved Poland's capital north from Cracow to Moscow to give it a more central position. His reign saw the construction of a number of early Baroque houses designed with gardens and defensive bastions in a single unified composition such as survive at Krzyztopor (begun 1631), at Oleszye, and at Wilanów whose architect, Tylman van Gameren, also designed the contemporary house and garden of Nieberów. Designed for the Archbishop of Poznan, Nieberów featured embroidered parterres which led into a formal lime avenue flanked on either side by formal woodland gardens, the whole bounded on one side by a great T-shaped canal. The most extraordinary of the French-style gardens, however, was at Bialystock, in the remote north-east of the country. The garden's parterre was decorated with so many stone figures, vases, pools and cascades, and its woodland held so many rides and pavilions that it was known as 'The Polish Versailles'.

In the early eighteenth century a Polish nobleman named Stanislaw Lescynski was twice elected king and twice deposed, ending in exile in France where he laid out the remarkable garden of Luneville. On each occasion his successor was a Saxon king and it was a Saxon architect, Szymon Bogumil Zug (1733-1807), who came to Poland in 1756 and introduced the English-style landscape garden. Zug's first important projects were for the Rococo gardens of Mokotow and Powazki. Both were located near Moscow and both commissioned by women, Helena Radziwill and Izabelle Czartoryska, who were to become the outstanding patrons of the English landscape garden in Poland. In 1778 Zug began a second landscape garden for Helena Radziwill at a place called Arkadia fifty miles from Warsaw.

Stanislaw-August Poniatowski had been the lover of Catherine the Great of Russia who, tiring of him, forced his election as King of Poland in 1764. He soon showed himself unexpectedly independent of her wishes, introducing economic and agrarian reforms and establishing a sophisticated, cultured court. Stanislaw-August's ultimate expression of his new-found autonomy was the summer palace of Lazieńki, south of Warsaw. Built on an island in one of a chain of three lakes, the elegant pavilion-like building looks out on a park with a full compliment of smaller palaces and garden buildings, including both an indoor and an outdoor theatre. Stanislaw-August gathered around him a cosmopolitan group of patrons and artists. Outstanding figures in the contemporary European gardening world were frequent visitors to the castle. Among them was the Belgian Prince, Charles-Joseph de Ligne (1735-1814) author of *Coup d'Oeil sur Beloeil et sur une grande partie de jardins de l'Europe* (1781) and Johann Muntz (1727-1798), the peripatetic designer of Gothic-style garden buildings. Many other parks dating from this interesting period in Poland's history survive, but in varying states of conservation. Some, like Muskau, Kozmin and Krzyzanowic near Wroclaw stood on German land when they were first designed. Stanislaw's deposition took place in 1795 at Russia's instigation. Russia, Prussia and Austria divided up the land between themselves and Poland was wiped off the European map for over a century. From the middle of the nineteenth century, general interest in botany grew and collections of decorative plants enriched the parks, some of which became remarkable arboreta. The Dzialynski family planted two important tree collections near Poznań in Silesia: Kórnik (1826-79) and Goluchów (1876-79). The rhododendron collection near Niemcza formed by von Ohaimb, and the two arboreta formed in the south-east of the country at Lançut and Krasiczyn also date from this period. At around the same time, formal gardens in neo-Renaissance or neo-Baroque style were revived to act as a visual bridge between the formal geometry of a house and the informal layout of its park. Two good examples of this development can be seen at Lançut and at Palanga (now in Lithuania) laid out for the Tyskiewicz family by the French designer Edouard André. An upsurge in the creation of public parks and botanic gardens paralleled the development in private gardens. The redundant fortifications around Cracow were taken down and a park encircling the city known as 'The Plants' took its place. The botanic garden in Cracow, (1798), and those in Warsaw (1818) were expanded rapidly in the size and extent of their collections.

The re-establishment of the Polish state after World War I, led to a heightened sense of nationalism. Parks and gardens were created around many national shrines, including the birthplace of Frederic Chopin (1810-49) at Zelazowa Wola. Designed between 1932 and 1936 by Franciszek Krzwyda-Polkowski (1881-1949), the founder of contemporary Polish landscape architecture, the garden is a blend of formal and informal elements. During concerts on summer evenings, the windows of the house are opened so that Chopin's compositions waft across the scented garden to the audience sitting under the trees. One of the most historic achievements in the history of Poland was the restoration of many of its monuments and cities after the devastation of World War II. Included among these restoration projects were many historic gardens, Nieberów (1948-51), Wilanów (1948-50 and 1962-67) and others were undertaken by the landscape architect Gerard Ciolek (1909-1966), who also wrote a definitive account of Poland's gardens.

The habit of bathing to improve ones health was well established in the seventeenth and eighteenth centuries. It normally took place in private, if possible in a purpose-built bath house located near a stream or lake. In the seventeenth century, Marshal Stanislaw Lubomirski built such a bath house in the hunting forest of Ujazdow south of Warsaw. Over the entrance was inscribed the following enjoinder: 'This house despises sadness, welcomes peace, encourages bathing, commends the country air and insists on propriety'.

In 1775, the bath house and surrounding estate were acquired by the newly elected King of Poland, Stanislaw-August Poniatowski, with a view to making them the basis of a new summer palace. Throughout all his subsequent alterations to the building and its park, he insisted on keeping the original, grotto-like interior of the bath house an integral part of the surrounding and on retaining the name 'Lazieńki' or 'Bath House' for the estate as a whole. By digging two new lakes next to an existing one, he was able to place the new palace on an artificial island thus creating what he liked to think of as a 'Palace on the Water'. The palace's façades appear to rise sheer out of the surface of the surrounding water, into which stone lions were set to shoot great jets of white spray. The rooms of the interior are filled with light reflected off the lake surface and the whole environment sparkles in summer sunlight.

The views from the palace down the lake are closed in one direction by a cascade of white water falling from one lake to the next and in the other by a Classical style bridge and a monument to Jan Sobieski, Polish victor over the Turks, which was built in 1788. From the banks of the lower lake there is a good view of an amphitheatre built in 1790 in imitation of classical models. The amphitheatre is faced by an assembly of Roman ruins set up on an island and some of the performances must have been spectacular. The court painter Jean Pierre Norblin depicted triremes — three-oared galleons popular in antiquity sailing towards the stage during the scene of the naval battle in the ballet *Cleopatra*, which was premiered here in 1791. J.C. Loudon, the English garden writer, recorded during his visit in 1813 that on special occasions, actors dressed in character were placed on pedestals and taught to maintain certain attitudes to form a living *tableau*. So perfect was their technique that the audience gasped when the 'statues' came alive and descended from their pedestals to take part in the performance. The park was gradually developed between 1766-1795 with the aid of the designer

Jan Chrystian Schuch (1752-1813). Schuch laid out a series of irregular paths through groves of trees to connect the park's ornamental buildings, many of which were designed by the Italian architect Domenico Merlini such as the White House, the Myslewicki Palace, the Cafe Trou-Madame (1780), the Orangery Theatre, the Gothic Orangery and the Roman Rotunda — based on the Mausoleum of Caecilia Metella on the Via Appia Antica near Rome.

Stanislaw-August's refusal to act as Catherine the Great's pawn once she had forced his election as King of the Polish parliament so annoyed her that she ultimately arranged for his deposition. In 1795 he was exiled to St Petersburg, where he died three years later. At this time the northern part of the country, including Warsaw, came under Russian control, and Lazienki became the summer residence of the Russian governors who built the Belvedere Palace above the main body of the park. Between 1819 and 1825, a romantic garden was laid out around the palace, including a botanic garden (1819). After extensive damage during World War II, the park was restored under the supervision of the architect Gerard Ciolek, and many of the present trees date from this period. Together with its palace — one of the most beautiful of its period in all of Europe — it remains a lasting monument to Stanislaw-August, Poland's last, sparkling but ill-fated King.

Klomby z gromadzone y sposob prowadzenia drog y sciezek.

A study for islands of flowers and a park at Klomby from the «Various thoughts on the Creation of a garden» written by Izabelle Czartoryska, Wroclaw 1808.

51

WILANÓW

The integration of house and garden was taken a step further in the second half of the seventeenth century with the introduction to Poland of the French Baroque garden. King Jan Sobieski, who triumphed over the Turks outside Vienna in 1683, made a summer palace at Wilanów set on the banks of the Vistula river outside Warsaw. The palace was designed by the Dutch architect Tylman van Gameren (1652-1706). French windows open from each of its reception rooms onto formal terraced gardens designed with the assistance of an Italian, Agostino Locci. Upper and lower terraces were connected by a retaining wall in the form of a *buffet d'eau* with water falling from a series of basin-shaped fountains placed along its length. Also connecting the terraces was a balustraded staircase with stone figures presenting a cynical courtly version of the four 'stages' of love — Apprehension, Consummation, Boredom and Separation. Another form of garden decoration unique to Wilanów was a stucco panel attached to one of the palace walls. Gilded figures on the panel support a winged Chronos, whose pointer tells both the time of the day and the current sign of the Zodiac. This curious and original device was the joint invention of the court librarian, Kochanski, and the famous astronomer Hevelius.

A sun-dial (1723-29) in moulded plasterwork on the south wall of the palace. The winged figure of Chronos — the God of Time — tells with his pointer both the time and the sign of the zodiac.

53

Wilanów
One of two heroic figures on a baroque pedestal on a lakeside terrace.

Clipped cones of yew give both height and evergreen accent to the newly-restored parterre.

Wilanów
An open temple based on a
design from Sir William
Chambers' Design of Chinese
Buildings was erected in the
English park c. 1805.

A mock medieval castle disguises
the very practical machinery of a
pump-house.

Opposite page:
A Baroque figure on a pedestal
marks the crossing of two
woodland alleys.

ARKADIA AND PULAWY

Arkadia
The flight of steps, designed by Szymon Bogumil Zug in 1783, leads from the lake to the Temple of Diana.

Pulawy
A design for a flowerbed taken from Izabelle Czartoryska's book 'Various Thoughts on the Creation of Gardens (1805).

Arkadia was named after the Arcadian myth which contains symbols of happiness, love and death; *Et in Arcadia Ego* is inscribed on a copy of the tomb of the French philosopher Jean-Jacques Rousseau which Helena Radziwill had made for an island in the centre of a lake. Srymon Bogumil Zug had designed Arkadia for and with Princess Radziwill in 1778 and had decorated the walk which encircled the lake, with ornamental buildings — the Temple of Diana (1783) with its sphinx guarded steps; the Sanctuary of the High Priest (1783); an artificial ruin built of brick, stone and iron ore and incor-porating numerous sculptural fragments of the Renaissance and Gothic periods; the Greek Arch (1785); the Gothic House (1785); the Murgrabian House; the Ruined Aqueduct incor-porating a waterfall and the Sybilline Cave. Later neo-Classical structures in the form of anphitheatre and circus were designed by Henryk Ittar (1713-1802). Framed by groves of trees, each building offered diversity in landscape and architectural view to the park's visitors. Arkadia was virtually completed when Izabelle Czartoryska commenced her landscape projects at Pulawy. She employed the English landscape gardener James

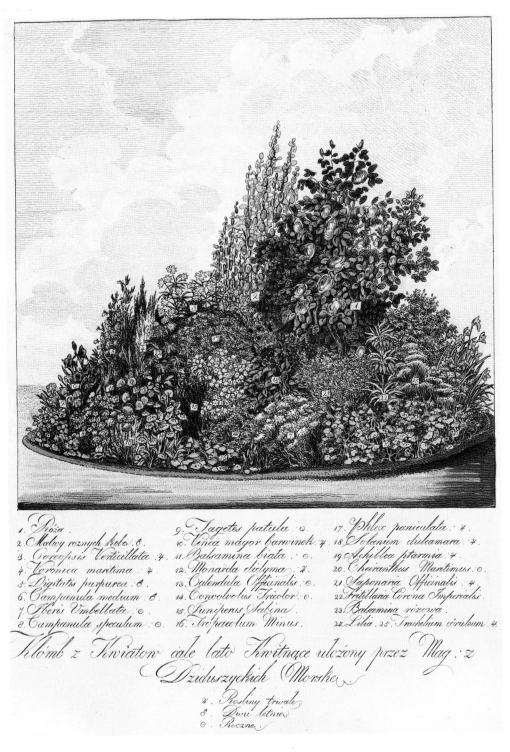

1. Roża.
2. Malwy roznych koło. ⚬
3. Coreopsis Verticillata. ⚬
4. Veronica maritima. ⚬
5. Digitatis purpurea. ⚬
6. Campanula medium. ⚬
7. Iberis Umbellata. ⚬
8. Campanula speculum. ⚬
9. Tagetes patula. ⚬
10. Vinca major barwinek. ⚬
11. Balsamina biała. ⚬
12. Monarda didyma. ⚬
13. Calendula Officinalis. ⚬
14. Convolvolus Tricolor. ⚬
15. Juniperus Sabina.
16. Tropaeolum Minus.
17. Phlox paniculata. ⚬
18. Solanum dulcamara. ⚬
19. Achillea ptarmica. ⚬
20. Cheiranthus Maritimus. ⚬
21. Saponaria Officinalis. ⚬
22. Fritillaria Corona Imperialis.
23. Balsamina rózowa.
24. Lilia. 25. Trachelium coruleum. ⚬

Klomb z Kwiatow całe lato Kwitnące ułożony przez Mag. z Dzieduszyckich Morske.

⚬. Rosliny trwałe
⚬. Dwu letnie
⚬. Roczne

Savage (1740-1816) and the architect Chrystian Piotr Aigner (1756-1842) to carry out the work, which lasted over forty years. A long drive bordered with four rows of linden trees runs from the gate along the top of an escarpment to the entrance court of the house. On the high plateau numerous groups of specially planted trees frame views to such park buildings as the Temple of Sybil (1798-1802) — modelled on the Temple of Vesta at Tivoli outside Rome — the Gothic House (1809); the Marynka Palace (1791-94) and a Doric-porticoed conservatory (1790). A marble sarcophagus (1801) reminiscent of the then recently-discovered tombstone of the Roman consul Scipio Barbatus rises on a nearby hill. The park below the escarpment is designed around a long lake set among magnificent trees. A number of rustic structures, such as the Fisherman's House and the Dutch House, once sat along its banks, but only the Chinese Pavilion remains. Many free-standing stones bear inscriptions, including one to the Abbé Delille whose poem *Les Jardines* (1782) had already made famous the park at Pulawy. The Czartoryski possessions were confiscated after the family took part in the 1831 rebellion against the Russian occupation of the northern part of Poland.

The High Priest's Sanctuary designed in a romantic vein as a primitive religious enclosure or temple. The effect of antiquity is reinforced by the incorporation of architectural and sculptural fragments including bas reliefs.

Arkadia

The lake framed in the arches of a double aqueduct from which a cascade of water formerly spilled. The Temple of Diana can be glimpsed on the right.

*Opposite page:
The rear of the Temple of Diana was designed by Zug as a neo-classical rotunda.*

KÓRNIK

The pneumatopheres or 'root knees' of the American Swamp cypress, Taxodium distichum, *spread stealthily in the arboretum's long grass.*

Opposite page: Clover finds a home in the flaking bark of Platanus acerifolia, *the London Plane.*

Between 1795 and 1922 when the province of Silesia was part of the state of Prussia, it became one of the centres of the Gothic revival and the associated style of picturesque landscaping. The first examples took the form of follies and park buildings such as Alteburg (1794) at Ksisaz and the Abbey (c.1820) at Kastrzyca south of Jelenia Góra. In 1831, the Prussian King Frederick William IV bought the estate of Myslakowice whose lake reflects the 5,300 feet mass of Mount Sniezka. He commissioned Karl Frederick Schinkel (1781-1841), the German architect known for his ability to integrate architecture and landscape, to build a church there, and would have considered a house as well had Schinkel not died in 1841. Frederick had to be content with his younger but not-so-able assistant, Stuler, instead. Before his death, Schinkel designed his Gothic masterpiece for the King's brother Albert. Located on a wooded bluff high above the Kamienic valley and approached by a long, shady drive, the great symmetrical castle overlooked a precariously perched terrace garden. Beyond it stretched the broad valley in which Frederick William had reconstructed a thirteenth-century wooden church which he had previously rescued from demolition in Norway. Schinkel worked in Silesia not only for the Prussian royal family but also for members of the Polish aristocracy. He built a hunting lodge at Antonin for the Radziwill family and remodelled Kórnik castle in neo-Gothic style for the great trade magnate, Tytus Dzialynski, who also established an arboretum at the same time. The arboretum was greatly augmented by his son Jan, and the collection of trees and shrubs today stands at 3,500 taxa. It is particularly rich in lime, poplar, birch, magnolia, hornbeam and malus of which since 1938 many specifically Polish varieties have been bred. The most notable shrubs are lilac, philadelphus, flowering currant, forsythia, deutzia and honeysuckle. There is also a well chosen collection of conifers. The arboretum boasts Poland's largest specimens of numerous species among them the Tulip Tree, the Maidenhair Tree, the Cucumber Tree and Grecian Fir as well as Chinese varieties such as *Euodia danielli*, *Eucommia ulmoides*, *Cedrela sinensis* and *Hemiptelea davidii*. Among the many rare shrubs present are the Caucasian *Andrachne colchica*, the North-west American *Oplopanax horridus*, the Manchurian *Prinsepia sinensis* and the South-east American *Asmina triloba*. In 1853, Jan Dzialynski bought the nearby estate of Goluchów and employed a team of Frenchmen to rebuild the Renaissance house in the French Gothic revival style popularized by the French architect Viollet-le-Duc. Lying in a valley wooded with ancient oak and beech, its English-style landscape park was, like Kórnik, planted with a tree collection which now boasts over 2,000 taxa, mainly of broad-leafed and coniferous trees.

Jan Dzialynski had no immediate heir and the properties were inherited by Ladislaus Zamoyski, who in 1889 was able to acquire an enormous region of Bukowina, Bialka and Zakopane in the Tatra mountains. Together with Kórnik and Goluchów he bequeathed these areas to the Kornik foundation which he established in 1924 and for which the Polish state took responsibility in 1937. The Tatra properties now form part of the Tatra National Park, the Goluchów arboretum is managed by the Academy of Agriculture and Poznań and the Kórnik arboretum are run by the Institute of Dendrology of the Polish Academy of Sciences. The latter is the principal research centre in forestry and the cultivation of ornamental trees in the country.

LAŃCUT

The gloriette's (c.1810) semi-circle of corinthian columns forms a focal point on a nearby hill.

Lançut, the greatest house in Poland south of the Vistula river, was developed out of the burnt-out shell of a fourteenth-century castle by the great magnate Stanislaw Lubomirski in 1629. On the outside, it was rebuilt for defense with elaborate earthworks, dry moats, screens and bastions laid out on a strict pentagonal ground plan. It successfully withstood sieges in 1657 and 1702. Inside, it was developed as a sumptuous residence with stucco by the great Giovanni Battista Falconi (1625-1660).

The last resident in the Lubomirski line married Izabelle Czartoryska (1746-1835), the great patron of natural landscaping in Poland whose work was eventually to be seen in no less than four landscape parks — Powazki, Wilanów, Pulawy and Lançut. She began her project at Lançut by levelling the fortifications around the house, leaving only the star-shaped moat as a ha-ha or sunken ditch to separate the new garden she intended to create from the surrounding parkland. The completion of the costly project was marked by the creation of the View Room inside the house, the newly-decorated walls of which featured a pair of oval-shaped paintings showing the house before and after the fortification had been taken down. Within the garden's new ha-ha she added a neo-Classical conservatory (1799-1802), fronting it with an Ionic portico. Inspired by a visit to the Villa Albani in Rome, she had the conservatory's walls painted by Vincenzo Brenna, the decorator who worked for Tsar Paul I at Pavlovsk near Leningrad. He conceived a *trompe l'oeil* representation of an Italian loggia in which painted sunlight filters through vine leaves to fall on classical ruins. This brilliant representation of the landscape of the warm south provides a formidable antidote to the harshness of the Polish winter. On a rise, near the north west corner of the house, she built a *gloriette* (c.1820), a half-circle of Ionic columns enclosing a figure of Venus on a pedestal which is no longer there. Within the former bastion there also lies a formal entrance court reached by a balustraded bridge over the moat and a formal parterre garden decorated with flights of steps, statuary and fountain pools.

With the assistance of two gardeners, Ignacy Simon and Franciszek Maxwald, the park beyond the bastion was developed in an informal scheme of winding drives and irregular groves of trees. Here also are many architectural features, including a small castle (c.1807) with a corner turret in the irregular picturesque style and a *menagerie* (1828-30). Much of the architectural work in the park was carried out by the outstanding Polish architect of the age, Chrystian Pyotr Aigner (1756-1841). All of this was idealized in a painted backdrop on the stage of Izabelle's private theatre which shows the park and its various buildings in a springtime scene.

Lançut

The castle's external aspect was altered in the French neo-Baroque style during early years of this century.

Lançut was inherited by Izabelle's son-in-law, Jan Potocki, who shared her intellectual and cultural interests. His descendant Roman Potocki and his wife Elzbieta continued to work on the house conserving the historic interiors but giving the exterior its present French neo-Baroque appearance. This latest rebuilding was completed in 1904. At the same time they built an orchid house, laid out a tennis court garden and planted perennial borders, all features redolent of late nineteenth-century country house life. They also added a rich collection of trees including excellent specimens of the Tulip Tree, the Caucasian Wingnut, the Maidenhair Tree (among the largest in Poland), the Lily-flowered Magnolia and a group of immense chestnut trees shading the house. This collection continues to thrive despite the severity of the climate. Alfred, their son, fled in advance of the Russian army's occupation in 1944, since which time the house, garden and park have been open to the public.

Painted sunlight filters through the vine-leaves of the trompe-l'oeil Italian loggia which was inspired by a visit to the Villa Albani in Rome.

Following pages:
The scenery of the private theatre was painted to represent the park in the springtime of 1912.

KRASICZYN

Opposite page:
The view from the park to one of the castle's corner towers which is topped with bartizans like those seen on many a fairytale castle.

Following pages:
The uncluttered arrangement of arboretum allows each tree to be appreciated as an individual.

The castle walls are painted with trompe l'oeil stonework with a frieze of grissaille hunting scenes at second floor level.

Krasiczyn lies in the south eastern corner of Poland near the Ukranian border in a setting of low hills and beech forest known for their gorgeous display of autumnal leaf colours. Near the old town of Przemysl the spectacularly restored castle, perfectly set in a natural, almost English park of rare trees, faces a lake which reflects two of its shining white towers. This present castle was built for the powerful Kraśićki family between 1592 and 1618 on a long established site by the Italian mannerist architect Gallazzo Appiani. It is constructed around a square courtyard whose walls are frescoed in *trompe l'oeil* depictions of saints, kings and other subjects both biblical and classical. Each corner is punctuated externally by a tower each with a different skyline and each named either after God, the Pope, the King or the Nobility. The outer walls, rising from a now-dry moat once fed by the waters of the nearby San river, are painted a stone-effect white with a frieze depicting hunting scenes above the second floor. The skyline is crowded with rooftop balustrades and dormer windows in a variety of architectural styles. The ensemble is viewed to best effect from across the lake, from which point the entire western façade glows amidst a frame of trees.

A causeway reaches across the moat towards an avenue which extends outwards through the distant forest. The 100-acre parkland was planted in the late nineteenth century with a collection of trees specially selected for the severe local climate by Leon, Prince Sapieha who acquired the property in 1834. Among them are the Shingle Oak, the Tulip Tree, the Umbrella Tree and the Weymouth Pine, all from the Eastern United States. Also present are *Magnolia kobus*, and *Thujonpis dolobrata*, both from Japan. Krasiczyn functioned as a school of forestry from 1945 until its recent restoration begun by the Automobile Works, Fso. The castle is still empty and its restoration continues. The park which no longer extends to the river and is reduced in size, is maintained with utmost care and has received a number of awards.

Krasiczyn
The clear waters of the newly-restored moat reflect a judicious blend of deciduous and coniferous trees.

Opposite page:
The furrowed trunk of a horse chestnut above a springtime carpet of primroses with the moat bridge in the background.

CZECHOSLOVAKIA

Czechoslovakia is a country of two nations — the rolling countryside of Bohemia and Moravia, and the broader landscapes of Slovakia. The recent farm collectivism and the subsequent removal of the hedges which divided properties, have given the Bohemian and Moravian countryside a park-like character. In both areas, the hills are often crowned with picturesque coniferous forests and the roadsides lined with fruit trees. The rugged slopes of the High Tatra mountains and the Moravian Karst region, with its fascinating underground caves and abysses, support floras of exceptional interest. In addition a unique man-made landscape of over one thousand carp ponds made between the thirteenth and sixteenth centuries survives in South Moravia.

No evidence of a permanent Roman occupation, and therefore of Roman gardens, has been found in Czechoslovakia. Neither does any evidence of gardening survive from the eighth or ninth centuries, the time of the great Moravian Empire. The only surviving architecture from this period consists of small stone churches, often round, one of which stands as an ornament in the park of Michalovce in Slovakia. After the empire's collapse in 906, Slovakia became part of the multinational Hungarian Empire, while the Czech nation consolidated around the city of Prague. Byzantine missionaries arrived, followed by Cistercians from Burgundy who, it is reasonable to assume, had gardens of herbs, fruit, vegetables and flowers like those we know to have existed in the monasteries of their homeland. The earliest written record of gardening in Czechoslovakia is a twelfth-century document describing the Diocesan garden of Vyšehrad, now part of Prague. The only physical remains of medieval gardens are the cloisters, with their stone well-heads and fountains as exist in monasteries like Zlatá Koruna and Vyšší Brod in Bohemia and Tišnov in Moravia. Outside the church, remnants of stately hunting parks exist, such as that created by John of Luxemburg in the late fourteenth century, and those in Central Bohemia at Karlštejn and Křivoklát made by the Emperor Charles IV about a century later.

The Bohemian throne was inherited by Archduke Ferdinand I of Austria in 1526. The date marks not only the beginning of Hapsburg absolutism in Central Europe, but also the introduction of Renaissance ideals and craftsmanship to Czechoslovakia. Ferdinand commissioned garden at Prague

Castle in 1534. In 1538, he began the erection of an adjacent Summer Palace for his wife Ann. Some years later he commissioned a star-shaped hunting lodge to be built at the centre of a radial avenue system in his new deer park at Liboc. The garden at Prague Castle saw further development in the reign of Ferdinand's successor, Maximilian II. Maximilian's physician, Pietro Andrea Mattioli, is said to have cultivated tulips in Prague before they became widespread in The Netherlands. His famous commentary on *Dioscorides' De Materia Medica*, which was in effect an inventory of all known plants, went through many editions and was translated into several languages. Mattioli's presence must have given immense prestige to the royal garden. Later, the court of Rudolf II was one of the most glittering in Europe and numbered among its members Copernicus, Tycho Brahe and the English astrologer John Dee. Rudolf employed the widely influential Dutch designer, Jan Vredeman de Vries (1527-1606) to add further fountains and gardens to the castle. His son, Mathias, added his own imprint with a great arbor which still stands in the south east corner of the garden. The impressive development of the royal castle and its garden during those years was reflected in the erection of a number of great Renaissance houses. Triple-arcaded courtyards in Italian style can be seen in Moravia at Velké, Losiny and Bučovice, the latter of which are said to have been designed by the celebrated fortification expert Pietro Ferrabosco. Single-arcaded galleries surround the gardens of Jindřichův Hradec and Telc in the manner of those Renaissance gardens depicted by the French engraver Jacques Androuet du Cerceau (1520-after 1584). The end of the Renaissance period in Czechoslovakia is usually reckoned from 1620, the year of the Battle of the White Mountain, when Hapsburg supremacy was again forced on unwilling Czech nationalists. Three years later, the Imperial General Albrecht of Wallenstein cleared a quarter in the medieval part of Prague to create the palace and garden which survive today. His summer pavilion and loggia at Jičín in North Bohemia also remain. Both gardens are in the transitional Mannerist style, much richer in its details than the Renaissance style but without the integrated composition which characterizes the Baroque.

The small-scale but integrated designs of the gardens at Kroměříž in Moravia and Troja near Prague are the best examples of the Early Baroque period to survive. The former was commissioned in 1665 from Filiberto Lucchese (1607-1666), an Italian working at the Viennese court, by the Prince-Bishop Karel of Liechtenstein. The latter was designed by Jean Baptiste Mathey and is adorned with statues and mythological figures by the Hermann brothers.

The true Baroque style — with its theatrical backdrops, its playful and sensuous composition and its often pompous monumentality — did not emerge in Czechoslovakia until the end of the Thirty Years' War in 1648, reaching its full flowering in the eighteenth century. Many of the truly great schemes of this time — such as those at Chlumec and Cidlinou and

Jaroměřice nad Rokytnou — are known only through paintings and engravings as the gardens were transformed into English-style landscape parks in the early nineteenth century. Lesser schemes survive. That at Dobříš in Central Bohemia, probably designed by Robert de la Cotte and with statuary by Ignaz Platzer, was saved partly because the landscape park made in 1800 was not around the house itself but around the adjacent fortress of Vargac. The garden at Milotice (circa 1720) in South Moravia, the complex architectural and sculptural detail of which is attributed to the great Austrian architect, Johann Bernhard Fisher von Erlach, who also designed the Parnassus fountain in nearby Brno, exists only because an early nineteenth century scheme for its transformation by Maximilian Erras was never implemented. In some places — such as the grotto-like *sala terrena* and the painted trellisroom at Jaroměřice — scattered fragments of the Baroque period are all that remains.

The end of the eighteenth century brought a reaction against the controlled elaboration of the Baroque garden in favour of the freedom of form of the English landscape garden and the restraint characteristic of neo-Classical architecture. The purest expression of neo-Classical garden design is the giant colonnade surrounding the formal garden at Lysice in Moravia. The best examples of the marriage of a neo-Classical mansion with an English-style park can be seen at Kačina in Central Bohemia and in Topolčianky near Nitra. The latter was once a Hapsburg estate, and since 1918 has served as a summer residence for Czechoslovakia's presidents. Later parks were adorned with ornamental buildings in a greater variety of styles. In the park at Veltrusy near Prague, which inspired the setting for Dvorak's opera *Les Jacobins*, there is an Empire summer pavilion, the famous Laudon Pavilion, a Doric temple, an Egyptian house with a sphinx, simulated castle ruins and a neo-Gothic mill. The magnificent park of Krásný Dvůr in North Bohemia boasts among its follies a Chinese pavilion, a Gothic summer house and an Empire-style tea-room. The greatest of all Czech parks at Lednice retains a minaret, imitation medieval ruins, a Gothic shrine, a Roman aqueduct and Triumphal Arch, a Moorish-style waterworks, and many temples and pavilions in the neo-Classical style. In times past it also contained a Chinese pavilion and a Dutch fisherman's house complete with quays and boat. Much of this aggressively eclectic architecture was created to satisfy the nostalgia and conservatism of prevailing aristocratic taste. This architectural exoticism was later to be complemented by plantings imported from distant corners of the world. Sychrov in North Bohemia became the home of an important tree collection begun by Prince Camille de Rohan. The widely-grown beech known as *Fagus sylvatica* 'Rohanii' originated here in 1894. Another collection of exotic trees was made in the park of Mlynany in Slovakia by Count Ambrozy-Migazzi. The well-known oak, *Quercus* 'Ambrozyana' and the arbor-vitae, *Thuja orientalis* 'Malonyana' were raised here. At Průhonice near Prague, Count Sylva-Taroucca tried to unite his collection of trees, perhaps the most important in Central Europe, with an idealized Bohemian landscape. The attempt was typical of the mood of this period, during which the yoke of 'foreign styles' was aggressively thrown off and native culture and landscape were embraced. The English style of landscape gardening did, however, remain in demand for the new public park movement, which gathered momentum throughout the nineteenth century as the population of the Czech cities expanded. The fortifications and moats which had ringed the old cities were taken down and filled to give ring-parks. Jindrichův Hradec and those surrounding Prague Castle (the latter designed in 1880 by F.Thomayer) are excellent examples. The success of the great spa towns like Marienbad or Carlsbad depended largely on the recreational facilities they could offer the patients between treatments. The gardens and parks of Marienbad, over ninety-six hectares, were laid out early in the nineteenth century to the design of Václav Skalník, whose work was the inspiration for a poem by Goethe. As part of the nationalist revival in the arts, both parks and spa towns were adorned towards the end of the century with wooden buildings and cottage gardens in Czech folklorist style. The creative use of folklorist elements also characterized the gardens Jan Kotěra created around his buildings in Prague at the turn of this century.

The diversity of design sources in use in that period led to a revival of the Baroque-style formal garden, the outstanding example of which is at Ploskovice (1852) and identified by the distinguished Canadian historian of Czech art, Brian Knox as 'the last despairing calculation of an exquisite order'.

A reaction against the nineteenth-century gardens exoticism, set in early in this century, as did similar movements in architecture and other arts. The Austrian-born architect Adolf Loos built new 'decorationless' villas in the suburbs of Prague, and in 1930 the German architect Mies van der Rohe designed his famous Villa Tugendhat in Brno (1930) which has been recently restored. These gardens have a spareness in design and planting that reflects the forms then emerging in modern art and architecture. In the 1920s the Slovenian architect Josip Plečnik (1872-1956) was commissioned to restore and modernise Prague Castle and gardens, and today both rejoice in his ingenious minimalist inventions. Equal wit and ingenuity is shown in the works of the contemporary designer Otruba at the new botanic garden of the University of Brno.

Czechoslovakia has also produced many talented plantsmen over the course of this century. In 1913 one of Europe's most famous rose nurseries, Jan Boehm, was founded at Blatna in South Bohemia. The Horak's family nursery and alpine garden at Bystřice pod Hostýnem in East Moravia continues to be maintained in exquisite order by the present generation. The garden of the Institute of Ornamental Gardening at Průhonice is being developed under the direction of Professor Jiri Mařaček into an extensive modern landscape of dwarf conifers, flowering shrubs and ground covers. This appealing relaxed environment also acts as an outdoor laboratory for the study of the performance of newly introduced ornamental plants. The University Botanic Garden at Brno mentioned above has an important collection of willows under the general direction of Dr Jindřich Chmelař, a world authority on these tres. The arboretum of the Forestry Institute, at Křtiny also near Brno, boasts an important collection of exotic trees in a picturesque lakeside setting.

Czechoslovakia has an outstanding heritage of garden history and sufficient examples from almost every period remain for the visitor to study and enjoy.

Dobrís
The curving lines of the baroque garden design are represented by flight of steps, cascades and statuary on a maritime theme. The garden was laid out by the architects de Cotte and Servandoni in the eighteenth century and restored by the French architect Jean Thouret in 1911. The photograph was taken by Margaret Rutherford Jay in 1924.

PRAGUE

The Royal Garden
An Autumnal carpet of fallen leaves, flowers, nuts and mushrooms covers the woodland floor of the castle park. The Royal Garden, founded in 1534 by G. Spati and the horticulturist, Francesco, for the Emperor Ferdinand I, was reconstructed to the design of P. Janak after World War II.

Prague — The Royal Garden
The Racquets Court was designed by B. Wohlmut in 1567. The original sgraffito or scratchwork decoration was restored in 1952 and again in 1971. A 1734 figure of Night by the Czech sculptor A. Braun stands before the central niche of the Racquets Court.

Set on a range of hills overlooking the river Vltava, the city of Prague abounds in picturesque architectural and scenic views. Founded in the tenth century, it became the seat of the Holy Roman Empire 400 years later under the Emperor Charles IV. Charles's pharmacist, Angelo of Florence, founded the first botanical garden in Central Europe on the site of the present New Town Post Office. Though there are no records of gardens, it is known that the hills below the castle were covered with vines and the town squares had wooden fountains, later replaced with stone ones. In the late fifteenth century, King John of Luxemburg founded the royal hunting park of Stromovka. The park featured an elaborate pavilion, which was reconstructed in the English neo-Gothic style in 1806 and still stands today.

In 1534, Ferdinand I founded the royal garden beyond the castle's north moat. This moat was eventually drained and established as a deer park. The Stag Moat, as it came to be called, was used until the eighteenth century. The garden beyond was designed by the architect G. Spati and a horticulturist known as Francesco. A Summer Palace was designed by Paolo della Stella and constructed under the supervision of Spati and another Italian architect J. Maria del Piombo, between 1538 and 1552. The roof, designed by the Viennese architect Bonifaz Wohlmut between 1556 and 1564, is in the shape of an inverted ship's hull, following the design of the roofs of the town halls in Padua and Brescia. The entire building has been called the purest example of Italian Renaissance architecture north of the Alps. The fountain in the garden, known as the Singing Fountain, was designed by Filippo Terzi and cast in bronze by T. Janos in 1564. A gardener's house built in 1552 and decorated with Renaissance *sgraffito* or scratchwork, also survives.

Ferdinand's son, Archduke Ferdinand of Tyrol, filled in the moat on the south side in 1562 to create the Paradise Garden which also survives. He also built a new hunting park at Malejov Forest near Prague. The park was entirely surrounded by a wall and had at its centre a star-shaped hunting lodge decorated with magnificent stucco known as the Hvězda. Rudolf II was the centre of one of the most glittering courts of Europe, and he developed the grounds of the castle to form a background for his many entertainments and 'marvels'. To assist him with this he employed Jan Vredeman de Vries, the leading exponent of Dutch garden design of the period. His designs were published in *Hortorum viridariorumque elegantes e multiplicis formae* in 1583, and his work became known throughout Europe. Remains of Rudolf's Lion Court, which featured heated cages for a variety of beasts of prey, fig hothouses, orchard and a pheasantry can be seen near the Riding School erected on the site of his Tilting Yard in 1694

Prague — The Royal Garden
The ribbon bedding and contrasting tree groups date from the post-World War II restoration. Formal bedding, well-maintained level lawns and slopes with a gardenesque mixture of trees and shrubs characterize the Royal garden which is today the principal public garden of Prague.

to the design of the Dijon architect Jean Baptiste Mathey. The last structure to survive from this period is the cylindrical Mathias Arbour built by his son which carried the emblems of the thirty-nine countries over which he ruled. Despite the crushing of the tumultuous Czech uprising of 1621, the Hapsburgs henceforth made Vienna rather than Prague their principal seat and as a result building and gardening activity at Prague Castle declined. The power vacuum created by the Hapsburgs departure was filled in Bohemia by General Albrecht of Wallenstein (1583-1634) and in Moravia by Charles, First Prince of Liechtenstein. Both profited greatly from the post-rebellion confiscation of the Czech nobles' estates, Wallenstein creating a duchy for himself in North-East Bohemia only to be assassinated on the orders of the Emperor who feared his growing power. He was, meantime, able to acquire a sizeable portion of Prague's Lower Town which he

The minimalist fountain in Mrakotin granite erected during Josep Plečnik's post-1920 rear rangement of the castle garden.

Prague — The Royal Garden

The traditional springtime view of Prague castle on its hill of flowering fruit trees.

cleared and filled with an enormous palace featuring five court-yards and a large garden rivalling that of the royal palace itself. The garden is dominated by a monumental loggia reminiscent of Raphael's loggia at Villa Madama in Rome. Designed by the Italian architect Giovanni Battista Pironi and frescoed by another Italian Baccio da Bianco, it overlooks a formal sunken garden flanked by copies of bronze figures by the Dutch artist Adrian de Vries. (The originals were carried off by the invading Swedish army in 1648 and are now in the Swedish Royal Palace of Drottningholm.) Another copy, this one of a 1599 Venus figure by Wurzelbauer of Nuremburg, stands atop a bronze fountain constructed in 1630. (The original Venus figure is now in the Museum of Decorative Arts in Prague.) To the north of the loggia stands one of the most prodigious pieces of rockwork in Europe with pools, artificial stalactites and stalagmites. To the south is a more intimate garden room frescoed with scenes of Jason and the Argonauts in search of the Golden Fleece. To the east a large formal watertank holds an island on which stands a figure of Hercules, again a copy of the original by de Vries. The vista is closed by the arcades of the Wallenstein Riding School.

In the late seventeenth and early eighteenth century, a series of Baroque summer villas were built near Prague. The villa of Troja (1679-1685), built after a design by Mathey, has a

The old castle moat was converted in the seventeenth century into a small deer park. It was thenceforward known as The Stag Moat, the walls of which are shown here.

Opposite page:
The former Riding School designed by J.B. Matthey in 1694 was converted into an exhibition hall and formal garden to a design by P. Janak in 1949. The rhythm of the flowerpots echoes that
of the building's arcades.

monumental staircase and gardens with figures of classical deities sculpted by the Hermann brothers. The villa known as Amerika (1712-1720), designed by K.I. Dietzenhoffer, has a garden decorated with sculptures from the workshop of the Braun family who provided some of Czechoslovakia's most outstanding garden statuary.

The hill below Prague Castle was transformed during the eighteenth century by the erection of a series of grand city palaces with gardens scaling the hill as far as the castle on its summit. The resulting series of hanging gardens is paralleled only along the via Garibaldi in Genoa. The most remarkable early examples, such as those of Vrtba and Lobkowicz Palaces, were designed by the Kanka family of architects. Many, such as the Vrtba and the Vrznik, contain allegorical statuary by the Braun family. Most also show high belvederes commanding extensive views over the city. Rich stucco or fresco decoration is also often featured. The loggia of the Ledebour garden contains painted scenes of The Explosion of Vesuvius, The Ruins of Pompeii, The Rape of the Sabine Women and other classical and mythological events. Perhaps the most beautiful of the gardens is that behind the Kolowrat Palace in Valdstejnska Street which is a tour-de-force of elegant Rococo pavilions, canopies, terraces, statuary and vases. Nevertheless, each of the gardens is interesting in itself and

it is fascinating to compare how each designer made use of the hillside slope to maximum effect. Some of the palace sites which do not have the benefit of the hill nonetheless contain effective designs such as that of the Černín and the Schönborn in the French Baroque style laid out by M.J. Lebesche. In the nineteenth century, the growth of the urban population led to the founding of city parks. Two designers were prominent in this movement: Jiří Brauerl, who laid out in 1833 the first park, the Chotek Park, and executed the work on the park at Letná Plain; and B. Wunscher, who provided the design for Letna Plain and for the former Kinský garden, which has been a public park since 1901. J.Václav Skalník, who earned Goethe's praise for his work on the public gardens of Marienbad Spa, created the first alpine garden in Bohemia behind the former Lobkowicz Palace.

The nation of Czechoslovakia, with its headquarters at Prague Castle, grew out of the collapse of the Austro-Hungarian Empire after World War I. The castle, a secondary residence of the Hapsburg family, once more became the centre of power and underwent extensive reconstruction under the direction of the brilliant Slovenian architect Josip Plečnik. He reorganized, paved and lit the castle courtyards and designed innumerable belvederes, pavilions, ornamental columns and obelisks in his inimitable, witty but minimalist

Prague — Wallenstein Palace
The two bronze horses lead
you to the palace entrance.

taste. During the same years, Karel Čapek, author of the humourous book *The Gardener's Year*, lived below the castle. Post-World War II landscaping in Prague has mainly been confined to the restoration and maintenance of its historic gardens with the exception of two outstanding examples of contemporary design: the elegantly understated former Ursuline Convent garden, now part of the new National Theatre complex and the more flamboyant setting of antique garden statuary set in an uncompromising modern design in the courtyard of the Lower Town Underground Station.

The palace facades are reflected in the surface of the great water tank which virtually fills one area of the garden.
A bronze figure of Hercules stands on an island in the centre of the tank. The arcades behind are those of the former stable located conveniently close to the watering for horses.

The Imperial General Wallenstein built a palace and garden in Prague to rival that of the emperor. It is seen here with the cathedral behind.
Bronze figures by the Dutch master Adrian de Vries decorated the garden. The originals, of which there are copies, were carried off by the invading Swedish army in 1648 and now adorn the Royal Palace at Drottningholm near Stockholm.

PRŮHONICE

Huge spruce firs echo with their pointed tops the spires and gables of Sibral's reconstruction of the castle c. 1885. A collection of ivies is featured on the house walls.

Three lakes were dug to create
light by reflection at ground level
and also to create humidity and
to speed the growth of
surrounding plants in dry
summers.

The estate of Průhonice was owned in the late nineteenth century by the Nostiz-Rheineck family, better known for having built Prague's Tyl Theatre where Mozart's *Don Giovanni* was premiered in 1787. In 1885 Marie, the heiress to the castle, married an Austro-Hungarian lawyer, Count Arnošt Sylva-Taroucca (1858-1936). Descendant from a former Portuguese ambassador to the imperial court in Vienna, Count Arnošt was later to distinguish himself as Austrian Minister of Agriculture. The newly married couple found on the estate a twelfth-century Romanesque chapel with frescoes dating from 1330 and an Empire-style house built by the Nostitz-Rheineck family. They commissioned the architect J. Sibral to unite the two buildings in one architectural composition, thus creating a huge castle complex in an eclectic mixture of styles.

At the same time, they employed F. Thomayer, designer of many of Prague's parks, to layout a garden around the new

entrance. Sylva-Taroucca himself produced a plan for the park, which at 260 acres is today the largest in Czechoslovakia. Using the many natural springs on the site, he dug three lakes with a combined extent of twenty-five acres. These lakes, together with the river Botio and its streams, create a humid climate that allows the park's numerous conifers to flourish through the driest summers. Rather than creating an English style park, Sylva-Taroucca sought a truly Bohemian landscape more in line with the Czech National Revival. Native trees were thinned to better allow the most outstanding specimens to develop further. New and exotic species were also planted — usually at the summit of hills so as to increase their apparent elevation. Count Arnošt planted many of these trees with his own hands — a gesture most uncharacteristic for a nobleman of the period. Twenty-five miles of paths and drives were laid, a romantic temple and seven summer houses were constructed and a series of bridges crossed the garden's numerous streams. In rocky glens Sylva-Taroucca planted climbing hydrangeas to scale the cliffs above, which sometimes reached heights of 200 feet.

Sylva-Taroucca was assisted in these tasks by Camillo Schneider (1876-1951), a Saxon dendrologist. Together they founded a dendrology society for the exchange of knowledge of plants and collaborated on the writing of no fewer than three books on the subject. Trees were ordered from H.A. Hesse and Vilmorin, the great German and French nurseries respectively. Schneider made plant hunting expeditions in the Caucasus and (in 1913) in China, which was just coming to be recognized as the single most important source of woody plants in the temperate world. The outbreak of World War I prevented Schneider's return; he made his way to the Arnold Arboretum, then under the directorship of that great promoter of Chinese plant hunting, Charles Sprague Sargent. Also at the Arnold Arboretum at that time was another Saxon, Alfred Rehder, author of the famous *Manual of Cultivated Trees and Shrubs*. They collaborated on botanical research until Schneider's return to the West in 1920. Průhonice was having financial difficulties, so Schneider headed to Berlin, where he wrote and edited horticultural journals until his death in 1951. By 1922, 200 people were employed in the park at Průhonice, and with this financial burden even Count Arnošt Silva-Tarouca's resources were not sufficient to allow completion and maintenance of his ambitious project. In 1927 he negotiated the sale of the estate to the Czechoslovak nation, which retained him as advisor until his death in 1936.

The present number of tree species in the park represents only 20% of what was planted during the first 100 years of the garden's existence. Yet 1,050 different taxa remain. 850 of them deciduous, the remainder coniferous. Of the approximately 7,000 rhododendron plants in the park, 75 are species and 64 cultivars, mostly hybrids of the Chinese species *Rhododendron decorum*, of which about 20 including *Rhododendron* 'Arnošt Sylva-Taroucca', were raised at Průhonice. Today the park's most impressive trees are the huge specimens of Spruce fir, *Picea abies*, Douglas fir, *Pseudotsuga menziesii*, Nootka cypress, *Chamaecyparis nootkatensis*, Colorado spruce, *Picea pungens* 'Glauca' and Giant fir, *Abies grandis*, which cluster around the house and line the wide vistas radiating from its terrace. Other noteworthy conifers include the original plant of the dwarf Bosnian pine, *Pinus leucodermis* 'Schmidtii' discovered in the early 1950s. Other special plant collections at Průhonice include 1,000 cultivars in the rose garden and 120 species and 1,500 cultivars in the

iris garden. An alpine garden covers a natural rock outcrop and a collection of wild Czechoslovak roses lines the paths. Since 1927 Průhonice has been the centre of the Institute of Ornamental Gardening, which occupies itself with the selection of ornamental plants for landscaping purposes. For many years the plants grown were disposed of after their trials and assessment were completed. Under the present direction of Professor Maráček, however, the plants are replanted after test completion in the institute's garden to demonstrate ways in which they can be used in landscaping schemes. The result is a contemporary garden, growing in extent each year, featuring some of the best modern plants available, all arranged in a simple, labour-saving and superbly-maintained landscape scheme. In 1955, the immense herbarium of the botanical department of the Czech National Museum was transferred to Průhonice, followed in 1966 by its library of rare botanical books. Průhonice today is now not only an important garden and park but the main centre of botanical and horticultural research in the country.

Průhonice
The park boasts over 7,000 rhododendrons, many of them of Průhonice's own raising including Rhododendron Arnost Šylva-Taroucca, named after the founder.

A slope with pink and white Alpine plants above the lake.

KONOPIŠTĚ

The Rose Garden — formerly the Baroque Garden — is the most magnificent point of the complex of gardens, parks, terraces and preserves. Some two hundred varieties of roses were cultivated here. The tower of the castle appears beyond the forest. Cast-iron rather than timber was favoured for the construction of late nineteenth-century greenhouses. Its thinner sections allowed more light inside.

The neo-Baroque statues, Work and Science, stand at the entrance gate of the rose garden. Photographed by Margaret Rutherford Jay in c. 1924.

Archduke Franz Ferdinand d'Este of the Hapsburg dynasty (1863-1914), the heir to the Austrian throne whose assassination in Sarajevo in 1914 sparked World War I, was a man of difficult and contradictory character. Always at odds with his uncle, the emperor, Ferdinand promoted the Czech cause within the Austro-Hungarian Empire, surrounding himself with Czech friends, buying the country estate of Konopiště in Bohemia in 1887 and marrying a Czech, Countess Žofie Chotková, in 1900. When the emperor refused to recognize the marriage, the couple settled down at Konopiště rather than Vienna, expending large sums of money on developing the house, garden and park into a setting befitting an heir to the throne.

The castle of Konopiště, dating from the fourteenth century, is situated on a high, rocky outcrop south of Prague. In 1716 it became the property of the Vrtba family, who in 1725 filled in the moat and commissioned a new gate house in Baroque style from the architect Franz Maximilian Kaňka and a set of garden statuary from the great Czech sculptor Mathias Bernhard Braun. All of these structures remain. Between 1893 and 1896, Franz Ferdinand carried out a Gothic-style remodelling of the castle with the assistance of Joseph Mocker and Franz Schwartz. Mocker, who was responsible for the restoration of Charles Bridge and Charles University in Prague, undertook the exterior work. Schwartz, the designer of the neo-Renaissance Academy of Decorative Arts in Prague, undertook the interior. Franz Ferdinand also transformed the garden and the estate, again with two consultants, Messer of Vienna and Rožánek of Prague. Between 1899 and 1902, he created an enclosure of approximately 500 acres for hunting, removing the farms which had previously occupied the area and planting it thickly with forest trees. Gamekeepers' lodges were erected in a local ethnic style and many deer and pheasant hides were created. He was a passionate hunter, reputedly killing over half a million head of game in his lifetime. Newly constructed roads flanked with millions of wild roses ran through the naturally rolling terrain, passing through woods, past natural rocky outcrops and spacious meadows.

95

Konopiště
Detail of the rose garden — the circular flowerbed pattern was a popular motif of late nineteenth-century garden design. In the background stairs lead to a pond.

The park's high water table and deep soils contributed to the rapid growth of the trees. An extensive lozenge-shaped lake was dug using a railway line to dispose of the enormous amounts of displaced soil. From the south front of the castle, the neighbouring hills of Chlum and Neštětice could be seen reflected on its surface.

Franz Ferdinand's mother was the sister of the last King of The Two Sicilies. Through her he inherited the d'Este art collection of the Duke of Modena and much of the outdoor sculpture which he was able to use at Konopiště. He also acquired a collection of garden ornaments from the Olbizzi Castle of Cataio near Padua including the Poseidon Fountain which enlivens a clearing in the forest. In another clearing a commemorative Way of the Cross had been erected by a Countess O'Kelly (née Vrtba) to commemorate the execution of serfs there after an uprising in 1775. This Franz Ferdinand augmented with a rocky grotto in commemoration of his visit to the shrine of Lourdes in 1905. Among Franz Ferdinand's many collecting enthusiasms was one for representations of St George, one of which he placed above Kanka's baroque garden gate. Figures of Diana the Huntress and of the Whipper-in with Hounds on the main terrace provided appropriate subjects for a hunting estate.

In 1910, Franz Ferdinand created a large terraced clearing to make a formal rose garden known as the Italian Garden. Balustraded terraces descend the slope, the uppermost supporting a cast-iron conservatory in neo-Palladian style and the lowest a romantic water garden. The central terrace held the rose garden itself. Tiered in three levels connected by grass banks, the central and largest section is focussed on the Cleopatra column in the centre and four neo-Classical obelisks with hieroglyphs in the Egyptian style in each corner. The upper level, semi-circular in plan, is focussed on a Rococo fountain from the d'Este inheritance, while the lower level is centred on a Rococo vase with figurative decoration. In 1913, the English designer Marcham was commissioned to develop a water garden on the lowest level. He planted it with waterlilies and hedged around it with large-leaved perennials and weeping willows in the early twentieth-century style familiar to us from Monet's gardens. Over two hundred rose varieties were planted and the entire complex was entered through a neo-Baroque portal flanked by worthy stone figures representing Science and Industry.

Franz Ferdinand was a patron of the dendrology society founded by his neighbours, Sylva-Taroucca and Schneider, at Průhonice. This interest in the society is evinced by the

The pond, a Monet-like water garden, was created in 1913 after a design by the English garden specialist Marcham.

For the first time at this period, bright tropical colour was available to the gardener through the use of greenhouse-raised plants.

many notable tree specimens on the estate. The largest specimen of the Czech cultivar, *Fagus sylvatica* 'Rohani', Rohan's purple beech, grows here as does a good example of the dwarf Scots pine, *Pinus sylvestris* 'Watereri', (always more appreciated in Central Europe than in England, its country of origin). There are dwarf forms of the spruce fir such as *Picea abies* 'Viminalis' (first described in Sweden in 1777 by Baron Alströmer, a friend of Linnaeus), and *Picea abies* 'Echinoformis' as well as fast-growing upright forms such as *Picea abies* 'Pyramidalis'. The fast-growing Caucasian oak *Quercus macanthera* and *Quercus cerris* 'Tournefortii', a variety of Turkey oak which originated in the United States, are also represented by handsome specimens.

Franz Ferdinand transformed Konopiště so comprehensively in his twenty-seven years of ownership that it is now one of the best representations of a twentieth-century royal estate available for study anywhere. It was in this setting that the Archduke met Wilhelm IV, the German Kaiser, to discuss their mutual expansionary interests in Europe on many occasions, the last being just four weeks before his assassination at Sarajevo.

Konopiště
An early nineteenth-century star-topped obelisk with hieroglyphic decoration stands at each corner of the rose garden.

The sculptural group of Neptune was acquired by the archduke from the garden of the castle of Cattaio near Padua.

*A circlet of baroque statuary
breaks a path line as it winds
from the eastern part of the castle
into the wood.*

JAROMĚŘICE NAD ROKYTNÓU

The church's tower dominates the house and garden. The restored parterre in front of the house leads into outer gardens in which the bright colour of island perennial beds is set against dark yew hedges.

Jaroměřice was an important cultural centre when Jan Adam of Questenberg (originally of Cologne) acquired the estate in 1623. His son was a music-lover and an amateur lutanist, and from his staff he formed an orchestra that was perhaps similar to the serf theatres and orchestras which were part of the eighteenth-century enlightenment in Russia. The most talented member of this orchestra was a footman, F.V. Míča (1694-1744) who in addition to producing orchestral and balletic performances was an accomplished composer, premiering one of his own compositions as the first opera ever performed in the Czech language in 1730.

Between 1700 and 1737, Jan Adam remodelled this Renaissance castle into a grand baroque composition with the aid of the architect Jacob Prandtauer (1660-1726), best known for the Austrian monastery of Melk. In 1715, he began building, as an integral part of the architectural composition of the house, the church of St Margaret, to the design of a different architect, K.F. Ipper (1682-1723). The church has an imposing belfry that dominates the skyline. It is built on a more monumental scale than the house; likewise, the terrace wall which separates the church from the garden with blind arcading and trelliswork is more elaborately architectural than the wall separating house and garden. This is an interesting variation on the usual arrangement in which the family church is architecturally subservient to the house.

An idealized view of the garden was painted by John Adam in the early eighteenth century. The Early Renaissance garden was enlarged until it reached the banks of the river Rokytnó and enriched with stone fountains, statuary and seats. Formal woodland and labyrinths extended beyond the river to a focal apex. Beyond the garden proper, straight woodland paths reached to the horizon. At some time in the eighteenth century, this elaborate layout was swept away in favour of a new, informal parkland layout, the long vistas being expanded into wide, loosely-planted rides.

During the recent restoration, a period of drought revealed the lines of the old parterre under the landscaped lawn. Using this physical evidence and the eighteenth-century painting, the parterre pattern of four quarters around a central pool was restored, each of the four quarters having a palmette pattern in clipped yew contrasting effectively with a ground cover of white marble chips. The garden is bounded by stone seats and statuary depicting classical deities set against an enclosing hornbeam hedge. Upright, *Thuya occidentalis* 'Malonyana' replaces the usual clipped yew cones to provide vertical accents. This simple but well-proportioned restoration provides a complimentary setting for Prandtauer's house. Many large Czech houses have a *sala terrena* or summer dining room on the ground floor decorated like a grotto or garden room.

That at Jaroměřice is entirely covered with painted trelliswork intertwined with a pattern of morning glory vines modelled on early Italian examples like that at the Villa Giulia in Rome.

A cool summer dining room is painted with a trompe l'oeil *trelliswork arbour and an intertwining morning glory vine.*

LYSICE

Emanuel Dubský, a leading
figure in the Czech National
Revival, added a neo-classical
peristyle or colonnade c. 1853
with a gallery in traditional
Czech timber construction to the
baroque façade of his family's
mansion.

Opposite page:
Besides acting as a frame for the
flower garden, the colonnade
provides a covered yet sunny
walkway.

Set in a sheltered valley among the southern spurs of the Bohemian-Moravian highlands is Lysice, a Baroque house long famous for its colonnaded Roman-style garden.

The earliest house on the site dates from 1540 and survives today as part of the present building. Some of the original moats have been partially preserved as well. The later Renaissance house (1615), still partly visible in the arcades of the castle courtyard, once had a terraced garden and pavilion (1666). The house's present appearance dates from the 1730s — the period of what is known as its Baroque reconstruction. Also probably dating from this time are twelve stone dwarves or gnomes representing the twelve months of the year — a common feature of eighteenth-century gardens. The garden itself dates from the time of Emanuel Dubský (1806-1881) — who was Governor of Moravia and a leading figure in the Czech National Revival. At the age of twenty-seven Emanuel constructed the neo-Classical peristyle, which acts as a frame for the flower garden and provides a sheltered walkway leading around it. Similar covered promenades had been built for Catherine the Great by her architect Charles Cameron at Tsarkoye Selo near Leningrad and in Paris at the Palais Royal, and have continued to be used in gardens up to the present, the most recent is in the garden of the Getty Museum in Los Angeles.

Dubský's interest in the Czech National Revival eventually led to his abandoning the neo-Classical architectural style and adopting a vernacular, arts-and-crafts style for the rest of his garden. On top of the Doric colonnade Dubský constructed a further gallery in timber with simple, fretwork designs derived from traditional Czech wooden construction. Dubský was a supporter of local talent, and the incongruity in style between the upper and lower levels is a result of his hiring a self-taught local mason, František Vašíček, as architect for the upper one. On the terraces above, flights of steps and

Lysice
«Carpet beds» of dwarf foliage and succulent plants which are clipped over during the growing season are rarely seen in Western European gardens today, but are seen in many Czechoslovakian historic gardens.

pierced balustrades in brick or half-round terracotta tiles all testify to this late nineteenth-century vernacular style. The period's stylistic eclecticism is underlined by the decorative use of a set of extravagantly-moulded terracotta urns.

The terraces are decorated with 'carpet-beds' — beds with dwarf foliage and succulent plants that can be scissored over during the growing season to keep a smooth, carpet-like finish. Height is given by some outstanding trees: the upright oak, *Quercus robur* 'Fastigiata', of which there are many examples in Bohemia and Moravia; the upright poplar, *Populus simonii* 'Fastigiata' and the upright juniper, *Juniperus virginiana*. There are also many specimen trees of outstanding size, including an enormous *Catalpa speciosa*, an immense sea buckthorn, *Hippophae rhamnoides* and a number of good cut-leaved dwarf Japanese maples, *Acer palmatum* 'Dissectum'. The entire ensemble is backed by a natural woodland park of over 70 acres consisting mostly of indigenous species.

Opposite page:
In the severe continental climate large gardens have extensive greenhouses for growing tender plants like fuchsia or spider plant which are then set out in long borders and vases as well as island beds during the summer.

BOTANICAL GARDEN, BRNO

Among the garden's intriguing design elements are the miniature gardens in which small alpines are grown on lumps of tufa raised to eye-level on metal poles so they remind one of hats on display in a milliner's window.

The alpine ravine whose dry stone walls are divided by randomly-placed concrete butresses.
The vertical faces of the ravine provide an ideal environment for high mountain alpines.
Along some of the ravine sides, the stones are laid in a horizontal rather than a vertical bedding arrangement to provide the widest possible simulation of natural habitats.

The 27-acre botanical garden of the agricultural university of Brno was started in 1967. Due to its originality of design and planting and its excellent maintenance, it is probably the most significant garden of its kind to be made in Central Europe in the last half-century.

The garden's south-facing slope gives a panoramic view of the city below and is consequently kept free of heavy vegetation. The landscape architect Ivar Otruba has designed a stylized torrent with numerous cascades and reflecting pools for this area. The expanse of grass is also broken with circular beds of hybrid tea roses, each in a single colour, and a prairie-like planting of daylilies, foxtail lilies, and ornamental onions and grasses in the currently fashionable style known as the New American Romanticism. In contrast to the south-facing slope the perimeter areas are densely planted. They include a 'quercetum' or oak collection, a 'dendrarium' or exotic tree collection arranged on a geographical principle, and an outstanding 'salicetum' or willow collection numbering 350 taxa including — in addition to the usual European and North American species — rarities from Mexico, South America, India and South Africa. Its value is further enhanced by a 10,000 specimen willow herbarium overseen by Jindřich Chmelař, a world-renowned willow authority at the nearby Křtiny arboretum. The perimeter planting also includes a teaching garden for the study of systematic and economic botany; a perennial garden arranged in thematic areas — horticultural, ecological and botanical — and a 'steppe garden' that allows students to compare the plants of the South Moravian steppe with those of other steppe regions of the world such as the Caucasian steppe, the Mediterranean garrigue and the North American savannah.

The most intriguing design elements include an amphitheatre of 'miniature' gardens in which small alpines are grown on lumps of tufa raised to eye-level on metal poles like hats in a milliner's window and the 'ravine'. The cliff-like sides of this structure feature stone dry walls and constructions divided by concrete buttresses in an uncompromisingly modern design, which provide a rich habitat for various montane plants. The 60-acre Křtiny arboretum of the University College of Forestry was founded by Professor August Bayer in 1929 with material from Průhonice. It lies in a windy frost-hollow north of the city and boasts a number of impressive assets in addition to its willow herbarium. Stream-side meadows of wild flowers and a reflecting lake provide focal points for a collection of exotic conifers on the valley sides which rise to a dark background of Douglas and Giant fir forest. Although many of the exotic trees at Křtiny can be found nowhere else in the country, native cultivars are not neglected. Examples of the latter include Sorbus aucuparia 'Moravica', a tree with

edible berries that originated in Moravia circa 1880, and *Viburnum pragense*, which originated at Průhonice in about 1957. The new forest trees at Křtiny are complimented by another collection — this one of dwarf conifers and alpines — in the garden at Bystřice pod Hostýnem. This creation of the famous Horak family of nurserymen completes a trio of plant collections that together make Moravia a most rewarding area for the enthusiastic plantsman.

VILLA TUGENDHAT

In 1928 an exhibition to stimulate interest in modern design and modern culture in general was held in the city of Brno. The event included the unveiling of a new exhibition centre and a scheme of apartments built to exemplify 'modern' principles. In the same year Mr and Mrs Fritz Tugendhat — he, the scion of a highly successful manufacturing family, she the daughter of one of the richest men in Brno — commissioned the German Modernist architect Mies van der Rohe to design a house as a wedding present to Mrs Tugendhat from her father. The site was to be a steeply sloping bank overlooking the town of Brno, its cathedral and the ancient Špilberg fortress. The couple had first seen Mies' work in Berlin, where since 1913 he had been designing houses in a simplified classical style based on that of Karl Friedrich Schinkel. The Tugendhats, however, wanted a more contemporary style, and the result of their commission was one of the landmarks of twentieth-century domestic architecture. Mies visited the site in September 1928 and on New Year's Eve the Tugendhats cancelled a social engagement to approve the plans.

In the house's interior, Mies articulated his concept of free-flowing space uninterrupted by solid walls but channelled by a set of free-standing screens. This concept extended to the relationship between the exterior and interior of the house and to the design of the garden. The main floor of the house comprises a single large space and has one glass wall, 80 feet long, which can be lowered at the touch of a button. Another wall is entirely glazed as well, but looks into a heated glasshouse or winter garden filled with tropical vegetation. 'When you have a white house with glass walls,' Mies said, 'you see the trees and shrubs and sky framed in white — and the white emphasizes all the beautiful colours of the landscape'. In the living area of the Villa Tugendhat, Mies made the garden his 'wallpaper', the everchanging colours of nature thus forming part of the internal spatial experience.

The entrance to the house is at the higher street level. A roof garden, minimalist in style like all of Mies' designs, frames a carefully-calculated view of the hallowed Spilberg Castle. The main bedroom opens onto a rooftop terrace articulated by a simple but monumentally-scaled pergola and semi-circular seat, both reinterpretations in modern, industrial materials of traditional garden features.

The deliberate contrast created by the architect, Mies van der Rohe, between the formal, plinth-like terraces below the house and the natural, park-like garden beyond.

109

ided to reduce each feature, includ-
ial elements. There was no aspect
not reflect this process of distil-
ction. Mies admired the way in
Lloyd Wright integrated his buildings with the
surrounding landscape by means of terraces, steps and walls.
At Villa Tugendhat he followed a similar procedure, linking
the Villa with its garden by a series of wide terraces which
dramatize the site's steep slope. The first terrace, on which
the living area opens, is decorated with concrete containers
planted with spreading junipers which appear to float over
the paved surface. A monumental flight of travertine steps
descend parallel with the house to the main terrace, which
is surfaced in white marble chips that match the white paint
of the house. Below it two further terraces, entirely planted
and faced with randomly laid rubble stonework, form a green
plinth for the entire length of the house. These plantings,
which have recently been renewed, are of ground-covering
sub-shrubs which hang over and soften the terrace walls.

They are traversed by an oblique staircase, also in travertine.
Like the rest of the garden, the arrangement of terraces is similar to that at Mies' earlier Villa Riehl at Potsdam. A wide
path, bounded on the perimeter with thick woodland plantings, encircles the central lawn of both gardens. At Brno, the
path is surfaced with white marble chips in striking contrast
to the green of the lawn. The lawn is in turn articulated by
single, free-standing specimens of weeping birch and oriental plane.
The Tugendhat was the last large residence completed by Mies
before his emigration to the United States. The Tugendhats
were delighted with it but were forced to leave in 1939, a year
before Hitler's invasion. During the subsequent period it was
occupied for a time by the aircraft manufacturer, Albert Mes-
serschmidtt, then by Russian troops, and lastly by a kinder-
garten, until its recent restoration. The villa played an important role in influencing the subsequent history of landscape
design, largely because it was the first structure to use modern
construction techniques to unite interior and exterior design.

Villa Tugendhat
*The stark, angular relationship set
up between the different,
descending staircases.*

*The high-backed, semi-circular
seat in tubular metal is a
reinterpretation in a modern
material of a traditional garden
design.*

LEDNICE

From the windows of the house, the view encompasses the flat and intricate geometry of a series of hedged rooms in the garden and leads the eye out into natural parkland surrounding the castle.

On the border between Austria and Czechoslovakia, the Moravian hills begin to die away and the landscape becomes flat and marshy. Reed-fringed lakes and sluggish streams engender an atmosphere of melancholy that is strongest in the early morning hours when heavy mists float over the water's surface. Here is Lednice — a 400-acre park studded with belvederes and other romantic structures.

The property was acquired by the Liechtenstein family in 1249 and their first contribution to the present landscape was made circa 1550 when Hartman of Liechtenstein dug the first of its many lakes. Yet it was not until the time that Charles I was created prince in 1608, that Lednice underwent major architectural and landscape development. This first period of construction is thought to have reached its conclusion in 1618,

with the wedding of Charles's daughter. Charles remained loyal to the Emperor during the rebellion of 1621, and was subsequently able to take advantage of the confiscation of the estates of the Czech nobility to increase his own landholdings to the extent that he became the largest landowner in Moravia. Charles's son, Charles Eusebius had no interest in politics, being convinced that the only purpose of wealth and power was the creation of lasting artistic monuments. Sadly, his own great monuments were altered out of recognition by his descendants, and are known today only through the eighteenth-century engravings of Johann Adam Relsenbach. These show an elaborate baroque mansion, designed by a pair of Italian architects, Giovanni Giacomo Tencalla and Francesco Caratti. A tiered fountain of inverted shells, dolphins

and swans in the present rose garden is all that survives of Caratti's work. The complex formal gardens shown in Relsenbach's engravings include scrollwork parterres, fountains and architectural screens, and no less than three green theatres. They were no doubt influenced by the Italian gardener, Manini who, it is recorded, arrived at Lednice in 1653. At the beginning of the eighteenth century, Charles Eusebius's son added a monumental stable wing to the designs of Johann Bernhard Fischer von Erlach (1656-1723) architect of the Karlskirche in Vienna. It features allegorical figures of the Four Seasons by the Austrian sculptor Giovanni Giuliani (1633-1744) and survives to this day.

Between 1712 and 1721, the estates of Lednice and neighbouring Valtice were formally linked by an avenue of trees. Many small alterations to the house and park were subsequently carried out, but the first important additions to the present landscape park did not occur until the end of the century. The widespread flooding was brought under control by a system of waterways and lakes constructed under the direction of Joseph Uebelacher. His pump-house, which can be seen from the house terrace, is in the Islamic decorative style. The vast lawns and tree plantations of the landscape park were laid out by Ignac Holle with the assistance of the botanist van der Schott who also worked on the park at Veltrusy near Prague and whose son, Heinrich, was later director of the imperial garden at Schönbrunn near Vienna. A whole series

Lednice
The formal gardens are given summer colour with tender bedding plants — sedums, begonias and variegated cordylines — and all-year-round height with pairs of obelisk-like conifers.

of romantic park buildings were designed by the architect Josef Hardtmuth (1762-1807), including: a 200-feet high minaret, a ruined 'Roman' aqueduct with a waterfall and caves, a 'medieval' castle called Hansenburg (all of which survive); a Chinese pavilion, a Dutch fisherman's house with a harbour and the classical Temple of Apollo (none of which survive).

A further large-scale drainage scheme was installed under the direction of the architect Fanti. The largest of the resulting lakes stretches as far as Valtice and is punctuated by islands with connecting bridges. In 1815, the house was yet again reconstructed, this time in the then fashionable neo-Classical style to the design of the Viennese architect Joseph Kornhäusel (1782-1860). He was influenced by architects of the French enlightenment: Boullée, Ledoux, Percier and Fontaine.

Top:
The design of the curvilinear greenhouse (1848) by the Englishman, George Devien, is based on the Palm House at Kew Gardens. Its long interior perspectives which were characteristic of the nineteenth-century conservatory are rarely seen today.

Right:
Cacti and succulents, natives of dry climates at one end of the conservatory contrast with the luxuriant foliage of sub-tropical plants at the other end.

Lednice
Clipped yew cones, stone well-heads, urns and pedestals punctuate the flat geometry of the yew-hedged gardens,

Opposite page:
The minaret seen reflected in the reed-fringed lake at dawn. It was designed by the architect Josef Hardtmuth.

Though nothing survives of this work, a series of his neo-Classical temples still ornaments Fanti's lake and the lower reaches of the park. The Rendez-vous or Temple of Diana (1810-12) for example, is a monumental triumphal arch based on Percier and Fontaine's Arc du Carousel in Paris (1806) which was, in turn, based on the Arch of Septimius Severus (AD 230) in Rome Likewise, the Temple of Apollo (1816) is based on Ledoux's gateway at Arc-et-Senan near Paris which was based on Piranesi's engraving of the Temple of Venus (AD 125), also in Rome. The Frontier Castle (1826-27) is based on Ledoux's neo-Palladian housing projects for Paris while the last of the quadrumvirate, the Temple of the Three Graces (1824-25), designed by Johann Karl Engel, is also neo-Palladian in style.

The final reconstruction of house and garden began in 1842. Prince Alois II had sent a young Viennese architect named Georg Wingelmüller (1810-1848) to England and Scotland to study the Tudor Gothic or Elizabethan Revival style of architecture which had been pioneered by architects like James Wyatt at Fonthill Abbey (1796-1807) and Ashridge Park (1803-13). The fashion for this very English style had already spread as far East as the Crimea with the Russian Prince Voront-sov's commission to the English architect Edward Blore to

Lednice
The widespread flooding on the estate was brought under control at the end of the eighteenth century by the creation of a system of artificial waterways and lakes under the direction of Joseph Uebelacher. This created scenic paths through the park.

A begonia grandiflorum in flower.

design his Villa Alupka on the Black Sea in the 1830s. On his return, Wingelmüller began to encase and enlarge the earlier house in this new style but died before its completion. One of his designs was used posthumously in 1855 for the erection of the last of the park's ornamental buildings, the neo-Gothic St Hubert's Shrine. Only one element of the newly-reconstructed house was not in a historicist style: the conservatory. Designed by the English architect P.H. Devien and completed in 1848, its ovoid section, rounded end continuous apex feature and solid base were all closely modelled on the revolutionary design of the Palm House of London's Kew gardens, which was under construction at that time.

The new garden was likewise based on an English model — a hybrid between the Elizabethan Revival and Italian styles, developed by Sir Charles Barry and used by him at Trentham, a flat, marshy site resembling Lednice. The formal Italian garden style was modified by the substitution of Elizabethan-style topiary and hedging for the stone wall and ornaments of the traditional Italian garden. The interior of each of the large, hedged enclosures was developed in a formal manner, arranging low yew-hedges around a central fountain, vase, well-head or stone figure. The design was filled in with those patterns of half-hardy annual plants in carefully-planned colour schemes which were also being developed in gardens such as Trentham, Elvaston and Chatsworth

in England at the time. These formal gardens were seen not as an end in themselves but rather as a 'platform' for viewing the adjoining parkland.

In 1809, a new model farm was built which was later used by the agriculturalist Theobald von Walberg for research in the breeding of improved farm animals. Many of his ideas were taken up and developed by the botanist Abbé Gregor Mendel (1822-1884) in nearby Brno who used them to develop his theory of heredity. A similar spirit of experiment characterized the tree-planting in the park and garden. The Californian nutmeg, *Torreya californica*, introduced in 1851 was planted here circa 1886. The Amur cork tree, *Phellodendron amurense*, introduced from China in 1865 was planted at Lednice soon afterwards. Many North American trees flourish in the Central European climate and Lednice has excellent specimens of such species as the Colorado spruce, *Picea pungens*; the Western red cedar, *Thuya plicata*, the pencil cedar, *Juniperus virginiana*; the osage orange, *Maclura pomifera*, and the black locust, *Robinia pseudoacacia*. A formal tree of local origin is the slow-growing Scots pine, *Pinus sylvestris* 'Bayeri', named after the founder of the nearby arboretum at Křtiny, Professor August Bayer.

Lednice gives a vivid demonstration of the varied tastes of successive generations of one family, and shows as well how successfully various English landscape and architectural styles can be adapted to the terrain of South Moravia.

BUCHLOVICE

There are many houses in Czechoslovakia designed by Italian architects, but only at Buchlovice was the client also Italian, Agnese Elena Colonna. At the end of the seventeenth century she married John Petřwaldský at Buchlov, a grim but majestic castle built in the thirteenth century to guard the approaches to the Great Moravian Plain. He built her a summer pavilion to the design, it is thought, of Domenico Martinelli on the banks of a stream in the nearby Chřiby hills. As is generally the case with summer houses, the design was a light-hearted one, horse-shoe in shape, single-storied on one side, with a balustraded roof line and a copper dome over the central saloon in the manner of a North Italian villa. Thirty years later the summer pavilion was made a permanent place of residence and a complimentary stable block, also

Statues representing children
welcome you at the main
entrance gate. The use of playful,
child-like subjects in garden
statuary was first introduced by
Louis XIV at Versailles.

121

Buchlovice
The entrance court, originally a purely functional space, was later given an ornamental fountain with surrounding box hedges.

in horse-shoe shape, was built facing it to form an ingeniously-shaped courtyard. In the 1740s decorative iron *grilles* were added and at the end of the last century, when the stables were converted to extra living quarters, steps were added and the horse-watering trough converted into an ornamental fountain. On the garden front of the house a *sala terrena* or garden room with pebble floor on which water could be sprinkled in summer to cool the room by its evaporation leads into the original small, formal garden. This has a balustraded terrace overlooking the canalised stream which was later bridged to give access to a much larger formal garden, 12 acres in extent, made by the son of the builder around a fountain decorated with *putti* playing musical instruments.

In 1754 the house passed to the Berchtold family, two Berchtold brothers transformed the surrounding land into one of the loveliest parks in Europe. Leopold (1759-1809) and his brother Friedrich (1781-1876), a co-founder of the Czech National Museum, were gifted amateur natural historians. Friedrich travelled in South America, wrote an Economic-technical *Flora of Bohemia* and made a natural history collection which is on display in the castle of Buchlov. Their elegant landscape of 123 acres crossed by winding paths and dropping to a bridge over a stream has an outstanding collection of well-grown and well-maintained trees. Now in their maturity, they brush against the house walls and overhang

Opposite page:
The park's winding paths lead past sculptural groups of trees. Here the loose, pendulous foliage of a weeping beech is contrasted with the dark, solid obelisk of oriental spruce.

the formal elements in the garden, integrating the formal and informal parts of the garden in a beguiling way.

Of the 319 tree cultivars at Buchlovice, many are of weeping form. Of these the most outstanding are *Sophora japonica* 'Pendula', which has grown an immense curtain of foliage near the house, and *Chamaecyparis lawsoniana* 'Intertexta Pendula', an upright species with numerous pendulous branchlets. Among the spreading multi-trunked specimens are *Pterocarya fraxiniofolia*, a tree with deep, picturesquely furrowed bark common in Central Europe and the Austrian pine, *Pinus nigra var nigra*. Tall conical trees include *Taxodium ascendans* — the only one in the country — *Metasequoia glyptostroboides* and the upright oak, Quercus robur, 'Fürst Schwarzenberg', which originated in the Eisenberg nursery around 1884 and is named after a prince of the Schwarzenberg family from nearby Hluboká nad Vletavou. Another local tree

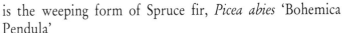

Buchlovice
The balustraded bridge spans the stream to join the old and new formal gardens.

The Japanese Pagoda Tree, Sophora japonica pendula, gathers its branches into tight, dome-like groups of pendulous foliage.

Many Czech gardens have fuchsia collections, the largest, over 600 varieties, is in the orangery at Buchlovice.

is the weeping form of Spruce fir, *Picea abies* 'Bohemica Pendula'

At one point along the winding path a narrow opening has been created in the trees to give a dramatic peep of Buchlov Castle on a distant hilltop. At the far end of the park in the courtyard of an orangery a collection of over 600 varieties of fuchsias are displayed. Ever since the mid nineteenth century when the first large fuchsia collection was made by Abbé Gregor Mendel, famous today for his theory on heredity, these plants have been extremely popular in Moravia.

In 1908 Count Leopold Berchtold, the then owner of Buchlovice and Austrian Ambassador to St Petersburg, offered the house as a retreat for Austrian and Russian Foreign Ministers to agree on the Austrian annexation of Bosnia and Herzegovina (now in Yugoslavia). It was one of the events which made World War I inevitable.

KROMĚŘÍŽ

Jacques Androuet du Cerceau (1515-after) was the engraver of a famous book on the châteaux and gardens of France *Les Plus Excellents Bastiments de France*, published in 1576. Illustration after illustration shows walled gardens divided by paths and cross-paths into a series of rectangular plots overlooked by surrounding arcaded galleries. The centre of the design is usually marked by a domed and cupol'd structure, often octagonal in shape. In some places composed merely of trelliswork, in others it was a solid structure, often with an internal grotto of shellwork, grotesque sculpture and amusing hydraulic devices. The châteaux of Gaillon, Blois and Amboise are all pictured by du Cerceau with such gardens attached. Sadly, none of these gardens remain. Only in Czechoslovakia, at Kroměříž in South Moravia, can a garden in the style of this period be appreciated today.

Situated in the fertile Haná lowlands, the town and Gothic castle of Kroměříž, ancient seat of the bishops of Olomouc, were sacked during the Thirty Years' War by the invading Swedish army. Few records survive of the castle garden before its destruction. We know only that Bishop William Prusinovský enlarged the garden, adding a small rosary between 1565-72; that Daniel de Vyskov, who looked after the kitchen garden in 1582, grew there the first cauliflowers in Czechoslovakia as well as a wide range of roses and carnations; and that in 1602 an apple orchard was planted by a canal which had been newly formed from a mill-race. The town's fortunes were magnificently restored after the war by a new Prince-Bishop, Karl Eusebius of the powerful Liechtenstein family, which in the seventeenth century owned more land in Moravia than any other. In 1652, Eusebius began restoring and remodelling the castle under the supervision of Filiberto Lucchese (1607-1666), who was at that time Imperial Court Architect in Vienna. Three years later the idea of transforming the old kitchen garden below the town and some distance from the castle into a pleasure garden was born. In 1666, Lucchese died and his place was taken by another Italian, Giovanni Pietro Tencalla (1629-1702), who was a member of the large Bissone family of architects and craftsmen employed by various members of the Liechtenstein family at this time. Ten years were to elapse between the garden's conception and its completion in 1675. By 1667 the enclosing wall and the pavilion had been finished. Over the following two years

The Summer Garden — a view from the arcade onto the garden with its central octagonal pavilion built in 1606.

paths were laid and lined with wooden palisades for training fruit trees, and two artificial earthen mounts were raised from the top of which views over the walls to the countryside could be enjoyed. In the subsequent five years, a 250-yard covered arcade in the Doric style was built along the south wall as a grand entrance to the garden. Each arch frames a niche in which stands a bust of a classical or mythological figure. Forty-six of them gaze out from their niches onto the surrounding Moravian hills. Finally in 1675, the stuccodores Q.Castelli and C.Borsa, the sculptor M.Mandlík and the fresco painter Carpophoro Tencalla completed the sensational interior decoration of the pavilion.

We have a good idea of how the garden looked at its completion thanks to an album of engravings by Johann Martin Fisher and J. van Nypoort published in 1691. From these we can see that its ten hectares were divided into two parts, one rectangular with the pavilion at its centre, and the other trapezoidal, with its pair of mounts as focal points. The rectangular section originally contained two labyrinths which were replaced by rose gardens in the early nineteenth century and a pair of flower gardens, one surrounding the Lion Fountain and the other surrounding the Triton Fountain. The trapezoidal section in addition to its mounts, also contained a pair of large water tanks. In the eastern section of the garden variety was provided by an aviary, a rabbit burrow, a pheasantry, an orangery and a Dutch garden. Remarkably, only minor changes to the original layout were made in subsequent centuries, most of which were focussed on the greenhouses. In 1722, the original wooden orangeries were replaced by more permanent stone ones; in 1770 a pineapple house was erected; between 1840 and 1845 the gardener's house and orangery were transformed into a hothouse. During the same period a new entrance court was devised, surrounded by a pair of Empire-style greenhouses designed by Antoine Arche. More recently, a project designed to gradually restore the garden was begun in 1954 under the direction of P.Janák, a specialist in historic gardens.

At the same time the garden around the bishop's palace was also being developed. However, it was to undergo many further changes before being established as the English-style park in which condition it survives today. During the years 1690-94 the original Renaissance garden within the castle moat was extended in the French baroque style with a vast parterre decorated with statues and fountains. Between 1777-1811, the period of Archbishop Colleredo-Waldsee, a landscape garden was created in the English style to the designs of J.M. Kraupel of Grunberg, Germany. A formal canal was given romantic overtones through the construction of an island and a Temple of Friendship on its banks. A colonnade in exedral shape

Kroměříž
Frontal view of the Summer Garden arcade — a 250-yard-long sumptuous and classical structure built in 1675. It covers the eastern side of the garden. Each arch contains a bust of classical or mythological figures.

was constructed in the newly-rediscovered Pompeian style and a small ornamental river was dug across the garden. Many smaller fantasies in the form of artificial ruins and belvederes were also erected. These works are depicted in a series of watercolours painted by J.Fisher in 1802.

Between 1819 and 1845 a final radical transformation took place. First under Archbishop Joan, all of Colleredo's indulgent fantasies were swept away and a new entrance to the garden was created off the town square. Archbishop Ferdinand Chotek then eliminated the formal baroque garden leaving only a small private garden or *giardino segreto*, to the side of the palace. He filled in and grassed over the moat, gave the mill race and river their present form and, with the assistance of the episcopal architect, Antoine Arche, made a dramatic enlargement of the park, creating vast lawns and planting many thick plantations, thin groves and single specimens of trees. The scheme was not fully realized until the time of Chotek's successor, Maximilian Sommereau-Beckh (1836-1853). Much ground levelling and modelling wascompleted, iron footbridges were flung across the river and the

small ornamental farm known as the Maxa was constructed. The tree planting, particularly around the periphery of the park was also completed at this time. In 1883, H. Struscha was able to name in his account 235 different woody taxa growing in the park. Through another major planting between 1913-14, this number, according to an account by Pavlák, was increased to some thousands. The deep alluvial soil had enabled these trees to grow to exceptional sizes, so that they now dwarf the architectural fantasies in the park. Of the sixty-three conifer taxa which survive, the most impressive are those from North America and Japan. A tall, narrow columnar Colorado spruce, *Picea pungens* 'Glauca', reaches for the sky near the palace itself. The more common species of hemlock and arbor-vitae grow in many Moravian parks but here there is a good specimen of the Carolina hemlock, *Tsuga carolina*, which is rare even in the wild. Moravia's only specimen of the Japanese *Torreya nucifera* can also be observed. The main character of the planting in the park is provided by the 290 different taxa of broad-leaved trees. Broad-leaved limes are the most common, and small-leaved limes are also

Kroměříž
In a grove bordering a meadow, a semi-circular Pompeian colonnade erected in the simplified classical style rediscovered during the excavation at Pompeii.

plentiful. Many of the older trees are of considerable size. The common ash, beech, oak, hornbeam, sycamore, field maple and birch are represented by many enormous specimens and groups. Against the background of these native trees many exotic ones have been planted. First of interest are those with Central or Eastern European origins: *Pinus nigra* 'Caramanica', a form of the Austrian pine native to the Carpathian mountains and *Acer negundo* 'Odessanum', a golden form of the American box elder introduced in 1890 by Rothe's nursery of Odessa, Russia. Splendid examples of North American species like the Indian bean tree, *Catalpa bignoides*, the Tulip tree, *Liriodendron tulipfera* and the Cucumber tree, *Magnolia accuminata* flourish. Despite the fact that the planting of the park has been simplified in recent years it still remains the most extensive collection of mature trees and shrubs in Moravia.

In the neighbourhood of Kroměříž, there are a number of interesting if less rich gardens and parks. The mansion of Holešov like that of Kroměříž was designed by Filiberto Lucchese and its gardens have a Le Nôtre-like monumentality of scale with an axial canal bordered by clipped trees. In the park at Zdislavice, there is a domed rotunda of neo-Classical elegance. Altogether the region of the Haná lowlands has an interesting family of historic gardens within its wooded and well-watered confines.

The Palace Garden — A
horseshoe-shaped staircase descends
from the archbishop's private
loggia into his garden.
When the formal garden was
transformed into a landscape
park, one small section was
allowed to remain — the
archbishop's private garden, a
ramped parterre on two levels
and enclosed by a pleached lime
hedge.

HUNGARY

The Hungarians, setting out from Central Asia, occupied the Carpathian Basin in Central Europe about 1100 years ago. It is an area of marshland and low-lying sandy plains with scattered beech and oak forests. Present day Hungary is no more than a third of its previous size since in 1920, through The Treaty of Versailles, about seventy per cent of Hungarian former territory was ceded to Czechoslovakia, Rumania, Austria and Yugoslavia. The regions's consistently sunny climate is particularly marked around Lake Balaton — Europe's largest freshwater lake — where avenues of oriental planes alternate with gardens of sweet chestnuts, figs, apricots and almonds. Hungary has over 500 medicinal springs, and in places such as Héviz, on Lake Balaton, the miniature tropical environment created by these springs is used to grow exotic water lilies in the open air. The limited use of fertilizers has allowed some spectacular displays of wild flowers to remain in the countryside. In February, great sheets of yellow-flowered *Eranthus hiemalis* bloom in the forests east of Aszófö in Eastern Hungary. The patches of alkaline soil near Szarvas turn lavender-blue each year with flowering *Limonium gmelinii*. One of Europe's most interesting scrub-woods is at Balatonarács on Lake Balaton where wild smoke-trees, *Cotinus coggyria*, grow among the oaks. Near Kecskemét, the sand dunes are a virtual juniperetum. Hungary also boasts many rare and endemic flowers: *Doronicum nendtvich*, for example, is named after a one-time mayor of Pécs who was also a natural scientist. The delicate *Crambe tatarica* or 'Tartar Head' can be found at Partflo on the eastern shore of Lake Balaton. The earliest evidence of gardening in Hungary is found in the ornamental courts of Roman villa complexes like that excavated at Balacapuszta near Veszprém. The young Emperor Hadrian, who was Governor of the Roman province of Pannonia (Hungary), built a magnificent marble palace at Aquincum in Budapest. It is reasonable to assume that he also had gardens there. Roman civilization in Hungary was destroyed by successive waves of migrants from the north, the last of which was that of the Magyars whose first king, Stephen, was crowned on Christmas day 1000. The early Hungarian kings had Romanesque-style hunting lodges in the forests around the Danube bend. Their palace at Visegrád was as impressive as that at Buda. There are no records of gardens in either place, but the hills of Buda were covered with vineyards even at this time. Great abbeys like Benedictine Pannonhalma must have had gardens similar to those in their mother houses in Western Europe, but again no records of them exist.

King Sigismund (1385-1433) possessed a royal garden, but it was only in the reign of Mathias Corvinus (1458-1490) that horticulture and garden design really began to develop. His second marriage in 1476 to Beatrice of Aragon, aunt of Cardinal d'Este, creator of the Villa d'Este gardens at Tivoli, brought about an influx of Italian designers and craftsmen. Buda Castle was reconstructed in Renaissance style with a hanging garden created over the great castle cistern and ice house. The historiographer Antonio Bonfini, author of *Rerum Hungaricum Decades*, Basle 1572, describes Buda Castle's lawns, aviaries, fishponds, gravel paths and fountains made of red limestone and bronze. The garden was also mentioned by Stephanus Taurinus in his *Stauromachia*, Vienna 1519 and is represented in engravings by Erhard Schon (1541) and Georg Hufnagel (1672). Terraced gardens, which included a labyrinth, were created by Mathias Corvinus at Visegrád Castle overlooking the Danube Bend. The red limestone lateral facings of an octagonal fountain remain here, and the figure of Hercules struggling with the Hydra, which originally surmounted it, has been removed to a local museum. The reconstructed Lion Well, also in red limestone, stands on a terrace above it. Its Gothic canopy shelters a basin set on the backs of recumbent lions and into which water pours from lion's mouths fixed above it.

The brief cultural flowering of Mathias Corvinus's reign came to an abrupt end with the invasion of the Turkish armies in 1541. From 1541 to 1686 a large part of Hungary was occupied by the Turks. Gardening decayed except in Northern Hungary and Transylvania where some late Renaissance gardens survived. However, Hungary owes to the Turks the introduction of a great variety of flowers and trees, including citrus, pomegranates, herbs, and tulips in many colours including green and lilac.

After the expulsion of the Turks, the reconstruction of palaces and gardens began. During the Turkish occupation of Budapest, Pozsony, (now Bratislava in Czechoslovakia), was the capital of Hungary. The garden, which belonged to Bishop Lippai, featured twenty-four symmetrical flower beds, over 150 kinds of flowers, statuary, a hermit's cell, a grotto and a water feature. An extraordinary book *Pozsonyi Kert (The Garden at Pozsony)* was published in 1664 containing a comprehensive manual of gardening in general, and is illustrated with several woodcuts. The Hapsburg decisive role in the expulsion of the Turks confirmed their dominance in the new period in Hungary. The first manor house to be built was at Rackeve on the Danube by the Imperial Commander of the United Armies, Prince Eugene of Savoy, who commissioned the Austrian architect Johann Lukas van Hildebrandt (1668-1745) to build a summer palace on an island in the Danube. Situated at the centre of a now lost Baroque garden, the palace was essentially French in style, but its rich external decoration also showed an Italian Baroque influence. Another important Baroque manor house and garden was built for the Grassalkovich family by the Hungarian architect Andras Mayerhoffer (1690-1771) at Gödöllö in the 1740s. Its wing surrounded an upper garden later recreated in the English landscape mood. The culminating work of the period was the great palace and garden of the Esterházy family at Fertöd, built during the 1760s. Engraved by Miklós Jacoby (1733-1789) in 1784 and described in detail in an anonymous but extensively illustrated contemporary publication, it subsequently fell into decay but not before earning the title of 'The Hungarian Versailles'. According to available accounts it contained long alleys bordered by statuary, a sumptuous cascade built by Franz Gruss in 1782-84, Temples of Fortune, Venus and Diana, three Chinese pavilions, a bagatelle, a zoo, a pheasantry, a hermitage and a music house.

The palace enjoyed its greatest period during the rule of Prince Miklós Esterházy, culminating in a visit of the Empress Maria Theresia in 1773. The composer Franz Joseph Haydn was retained as the palace's musical director in 1761, and between 1770 and 1790 at least one opera performance was given each month. Although extensive damage occured during World War II, both palace and garden are under active restoration. To counterbalance the Hapsburg Imperial power, many Hungarian noblemen looked to the more liberal world of England for inspiration. The English Enlightenment of the eighteenth century laid great stress on the value of agricultural and economic improvement for the population as a whole, as well as the need for education and medical and social care. Count György Festetics founded Europe's first agricultural college and laid out an English-style garden at Keszthely on Lake Balaton. Count István Széchenyi, the great political reformer and enthusiastic anglophile, redesigned his Baroque house and garden at Nagycenk in the simpler neo-Classical style and added an English garden. The period's preeminent landscape gardener was Bernhard Petri. Born in Germany, Petri studied in England before coming to Hungary in 1793. He laid out parks at Hédervár, Vedrod, and the Orczy Park, Budapest and Lednice in Czechoslovakia. Another German landscape gardener, Christian Heinrich Nebbien (1778-1841), laid out a landscape garden for the Brunswick family at Martonvasár and won a competition for the design of Városliget, Budapest's City Park, in 1817. The fashion for the English landscape garden was strongly promoted by Ferenc Kazinczy (1759-1831) 'the Hungarian Goethe', who was an enthusiast for the style. An exotic mixture of ornamental park buildings was erected; the three Esterházy estates were particularly notable for such structures. Kismárton (now Eisenstadt in Austria) had a monument by Antonio Canova in its so-called Leopoldic Temple, a collection of over 3,000 different plants cared for by a gardener named Anton Niermeyer and the largest park in Hungary designed by Charles de Moreau. Tata, near Budapest, boasted a 240-hectare park with a lake created by J. Mikoviny, artificial ruins designed by de Moreau, and a Turkish tent and Chinese pavilion. Csákvár also possessed a Turkish tent and Chinese pavilion, in addition to an Egyptian pavilion and pyramid and a classical temple. Although both the house and garden at Csákvár were ruined by an earthquake in 1810, a series of nine gouaches by Pietro Rivetti show the garden as it was in 1783.

The naturalization of exotic plants became common in the middle of the nineteenth century, particularly on estates with a favourable microclimate resulting from previous land drainage and shelter planting. Pioneer work was carried out by Count Sándor Erdödy at Vep in Western Hungary. His example was followed by Count Sándor Vigyázó, who willed his estate at Vacrotot to the Hungarian Academy of Sciences. In 1890, Count Pál Bolza began a collection of trees at Szarvas on the Great Plain which now forms one of the most interesting sites in the arboretal chain of Europe. In 1891, Count István Saághy began the arboretum of Kamon which still contains one of the richest collection of trees in Western Hungary. Towards the end of the century the rich bourgeoisie and the intelligentsia began building villas in the clean air of the Buda Hills, often surrounding them with large gardens and interesting plant collections. The most notable of these belonged to Vilmos Manninger. The nineteenth century was a period of many conections between England and Hungary.

The cultural links established between the two countries bore fruit in a Hungarian Arts and Crafts Movement based on that started by William Morris. The park-like settings of the artist's colonies at Szolnok and Gödöllö are excellent examples of the attempt to integrate art and life into an idealized landscape setting.

Today the tradition of establishing and maintaining arboreta continues. New ones have been created at Tiszakürti on the Great Plain and Malamvölgy in the South, while Mr Gyula Folly continues to maintain the jewel-like collection of trees established by his grandfather on a hillside at Badacsony on Lake Balaton. The botanic gardens have been established in Budapest since 1945. The fifty-six-hectare Soroksár Botanic Garden south of the city was geographically designed by Professor András Terpo over twenty-five years ago. Terpo was also responsible for the seven-hectare garden of the University of Horticulture located on the Buda Hills. The restoration of historic gardens such as Nagycenk, Esterháza, Tata and Martonvásár is a continuing activity while the contemporary landscape profession is perhaps best represented by the distinguished János Máthé, who has worked extensively in Hungary and abroad.

While Hungary has a tradition of gardening that spans most of the great gardening periods in Europe, its richest heritage is in the landscape parks of the late eighteenth and early nineteenth centuries and in its outstanding arboreta which date from approximately a century later.

ESTERHÁZA

«The Hungarian Versailles» — the entrance courtyard has curving wings and a curving drive to enable carriages to draw up at speed.

Like many Catholic nobles, the Esterházy family remained loyal to the Catholic Hapsburg throne during the notoriously unsuccessful Hungarian War of Independence (1703-11). As reward for their loyalty, in 1719, they were given an extensive group of confiscated estates in Eastern Hungary, including the estate at Fertőd, where soon after Prince Antal Esterházy built a hunting lodge to the design of the Vienna based Italian architect Anton Erhard Martinelli (circa 1684-1747). An anonymous painting from the early eighteenth century gives a bird's eye view of the lodge and shows it already surrounded by the framework of the present garden, its parterre, formal plantations and alleys extending to the horizon. Esterháza, as it was now called, did not truly enter its great period until 1756, when Prince Miklós Esterházy, known as 'The Magnificent', commissioned designs for the property from Melchior Hefele (1716-1799), the drawing master of the Hungarian Guards in Vienna. The Prince intended to transform Esterháza from a relatively modest hunting lodge into a grand summer palace based, in its massing and arrangements, on the imperial summer palace of Schönbrunn near Vienna. Despite the fact that he was simultaneously engaged in reconstructing his family's main house at Kismarton (now Eisenstadt in Austria), the Prince's attentions were largely directed to the summer palace. A huge inventory of works was initiated when in 1762 he added the guard houses and guest quarters; in 1764 a pair of horseshoe-shaped wings designed by Johann Ferdinand Mödlhammer, in 1765 a tripartite set of iron entry-gates crowned with garlands of flowers by Karl Johann Franke; in 1768 an opera house, in 1769 a music building to house his actors and musicians, in 1772 garden temples to Venus and Fortune and a Triumphal arch in the park, and in 1773 a puppet theatre.

This steady accumulation culminated in the visit of the Empress Maria Theresia in September of 1773, an event for which Franz Joseph Haydn, the Prince's court musician who had composed 700 pieces since his arrival in 1761, created two new operas. The Empress was suitably impressed by everything — particularly the new Chinese pavilion which had been built especially for her visit — and could not resist questioning the Prince on how much this structure had cost. He replied that 'It is but a bagatelle (a trifle)', and from then on 'The Bagatelle' was the name the pavilion went by.

Each summer the prince, an ambitious and prestigious personality of European aristocracy, hosted sumptuous entertainment at Esterháza modelled on events at Versailles. These mainly took place in the garden, the overall plan of which was based on a plate in André Mollet's book *Le Jardin de Plaisir* (1651). Each panel of this parterre garden was edged with a band of mixed flowers, while the paths were lined with no fewer than

twenty sandstone vases, thirty-two sculptures, sixty-eight orange trees in cases and seventy-six flower baskets. In addition, the crossings were marked with fountains.

Beyond the parterre stretched a formal woodland garden of clipped trees crossed by oak, chestnut and linden alleys, at the various crossings of which stood temples to Diana and Apollo. Also present were a Chinese pavilion crowned with a Chinaman holding an umbrella like the one at Sans Souci, a thorn-fenced hermitage, trick fountains, rose gardens and a fireworks arena. The garden came to an end before a half-circle of linden trees and a triumphal arch led from there into an 820-acre deer park. A pair of ornamental cascades, designed by Franz Gruss in 1784, completed the scene. The deer park was also crossed and recrossed by alleys, down which a twelve-wheeled carriages, furnished inside with a table and chairs,

A detail of a one of the French windows which opens directly from the principal rooms into the garden to allow them to be used interdependently.

Following pages:
The repetitive rhythm of the windows is echoed in the clipped yew cones which date from the 1950's restoration.

would carry the elderly guests and those not given to riding on horseback. A neighbouring park for boar-hunting was designed as an *étoile* of avenues radiating from a central *rond-point* in the French manner.

By the 1780s, the garden's reputation was such that it was frequently described and illustrated. Its elaborate plan decorated the back of a fan from this period now in the Museum of the History of the Theatre in Budapest. In 1781 Caetano Peici painted a bird's eye view of the parterre. In 1783 a German traveller, Gottfried von Rothenstein, enthusiastically described the enclosed gardens of orange trees in wooden

Esterháza
Carpet-like panels of grass in the entrance court have scroll-like decorations of flowers and coloured sand.

A detail of cherubs hanging garlands of flowers along the roof balustrade in a decoration common in the seventeenth century.

The main triple entrance gates made by Johann Karl Franke are surmounted by a cornucopia of wrought iron flowers, fruit, foliage executed in realistic detail greeting visitors as they walk through to the palace.

Detail of a basket of flowers from the main gate.

Esterháza
A pavilion on the entrance courtyard

cases near the palace. 1784 saw the publication of a lavish book describing every aspect of the garden. Engravings in the manner of Lepautre 1710 depictions of the garden at Versailles were carried out for the edition by Miklós Jacoby (1733-1784), an architect who had been involved with the Prince's building activities for over thirty years.

With the Prince's death in 1790 this glorious period came to an end. The orchestra was dispersed, the theatres shut up and the furnishings and pictures moved back to Kismarton. Within twenty-five years, the house had become a ruin, with sheep being kept on the ground floor rooms and potatoes growing on what formerly had been closely manicured lawns.

Even before the Prince's death the elaborate garden for court entertainment was outmoded and the Esterházy family had begun gardens in the more private, contemplative, English style which was to become fashionable in Hungary in the succeeding half-century. By 1781 such a garden had been made at Csákvár, an Esterházy estate outside Budapest. Pietro Rivetti's nine gouaches show park buildings as they were in 1783 — a hilltop eye-catcher, an Egyptian pyramid, a Turkish tent and a Temple of Apollo. All of these, along with the main house, were destroyed by an earthquake in 1810.

The family had further estates at Tata, Kismarton, Szigliget on Lake Balaton, Cseklesz (now Bernolakova) and Sárosd, all of which had English parks from about 1820. The various houses, parks and gardens initiated by the Esterházy family form a significant contribution to the architectural and garden heritage of Central Europe — a contribution which is being recognized by the lengthy and costly project now under way to repair the enormous damage done to Esterháza in the final days of World War II.

Lithograph giving a view of the garden and the Villa in 1784 — Courtesy of the Hungarian National Museum.

NAGYCENK

View from the linden avenue, planted by Zsuzsanna Szechényi c. 1750, towards the early nineteenth-century house façade.

The wrought-iron balcony's scroll-like pattern is repeated in the pattern of the parterre which ends where the linden avenue starts.

144

Nagycenk
*The severe, neo-classical design of
one of the garden gates leading
into the parterre.*

*Opposite page:
The clear stem of a specimen of
Prunus Mohacs marks the
entrance to one of the high-hedged
walks of the sunken pool garden.*

Nagycenk is situated in low-lying marsh area around Lake Fertöd where in 1529 the difficult ground conditions thwarted Suleiman the Magnificent's advance on Vienna. Its broad pasture lands lined with magnificent trees support the horses of one of Hungary's most famous stud farms. The property was bought by the Széchenyi family in 1711, who built the first house on the present site in 1741. No fewer than three plans for a formal garden in the Viennese baroque style, all tentatively dated to the 1760s, survive in the Budapest National Archives. The first is an anonymous plan for a rectilinear parterre flanked with formal green rooms; the second, by Caspar Kollman, is a trapezoidal parterre flanked by an orchard and kitchen garden; the third, by Kneidinger is a combination of the first two, and is the one that was ultimately adopted. In size and general arrangements, the plan seems more suitable for a town than a country garden and bears a family resemblance to the garden of the Palais Schwarzenberg in Vienna. What remains of this garden is the two-mile-long linden avenue, planted by Antal Széchenyi's wife Zsuzsanna, that stretches gloriously from the parterre in front

of the house to join the horizon. Antal's son, Ferenc (1754-1820), was the brother in law of the agricultural and educational reformer Count György Festetics (1755-1819), and himself a noted collector and philantropist who founded the Hungarian National Museum. Ferenc inherited Nagycenk in 1767, took up residence there in 1783, and soon set about improving first his garden and then the house.

Three plans also survive in the Budapest National Archives from this period; the first is an anonymous project drawn soon after he moved into the house showing his father's baroque garden still in place; the second, also anonymous, shows an English design created around the garden while the third, by the surveyor András Hegedius, shows the baroque garden entirely swept away and supplanted by one in an English style. Like both his father and his son, Ferenc excluded fashionable Viennese architects in favour of local talent, in his case József Ringer of the nearby town of Sopron. Ringer designed a *gloriette* or domed rotunda on a hill in the park to commemorate the visit of Palatine József in 1802 and an octagonal family mausoleum in 1806 with a neo-Classical front added in 1810.

Ferenc's son, István (1791-1860) travelled in England from 1815 to 1816, returning with an English-born wife, Crescencia Seilern. István is remembered for a number of achievements: he founded the Hungarian Academy of Sciences, introduced a number of innovations to his country from England in such fields as domestic comforts, horse-breeding, general transport and communications, and was an heroic political activist. His innovations such as at Nagycenk are less well known but equally impressive. He gave over half his agricultural land to his serfs, draining much of it and creating a model, progressive farm. Like many enlightened patrons, he passed from a predilection for the neo-Classical architectural style having enlarged his house in 1834-40, to one for the National Romantic style.

In 1860 Nagycenk was inherited by his son Béla. During the 1860s and 1870s, Béla erected the present cast-iron conservatory and added a number of rare trees to the already huge plane trees in the park including Caucasian wingnut, *Pterocarya fraxinifolia*, sweet buckeye, *Aesculus flava*, Tricolour sycamore, *Acer pseudoplatanus* 'Leopoldii'; Welling-tonia, *Sequoiadendron giganteum*; the Kentucky Coffee tree, *Gymnocladus dioica*; purple beech, tulip and maidenhair trees. Béla and his wife are commemorated by a mausoleum designed by Karoly Kurdmann erected in place of the late-eighteenth-century grotto at the end of the linden avenue and surrounded by Caucasian fir, *Abies nordmanniana*.

The garden remained close to Ferenc Széchenyi's design of 1789 up until the end of World War II at which point it suffered severe damage. Unfortunately Ferenc's plans were not rediscovered until after the restoration of the garden was undertaken. Nevertheless the scale, if not the detail, of the present design is faithful to Ferenc's design. The box parterre with intricate scrolls and volutes, ending in a jet of sparkling water, is flanked by aerial hedges of the local cherry trees, *Prunus mohacs* (called after a Hungarian fruit-tree expert), clipped not in a continuous hedge but in a series of balls in the manner of eighteenth-century Russian models. The main house and garden have been open to the public since 1973 and receive tens of thousands of visitors each year.

BOTANIC GARDENS

Budapest Botanic Gardens
Wisteria flowers over an arbour attached to one of the garden's buildings.

Flora Tyrnavensis, the first local Hungarian flora, was written in 1774 under the direction of Jakab Winterl. Winterl was then professor of botany at what is now the Loránd Eötvös University which was founded in 1636 at Trnava (now in Czechoslovakia). In 1777 the university moved to Buda, and then in 1784 to Pest. Known as the Royal Botanic Garden, its most eminent director was Pál Kitaibel (1757-1817) who wrote extensively on Hungarian plants in collaboration with a Viennese officer and amateur botanist, Count Franz von Waldenstein-Wartenberg (1759-1854). In 1847 the garden moved to its present site, the English park of a villa designed for the Festetics family by Mihály Pollak (1773-1855) in 1809. The extension of Pest has reduced the park's size, but it still holds approximately 6,000 taxa. The early-nineteenth-century neo-Classical glasshouse, the palm house, in which the *Victoria regia* water lily is grown, and the busts of several Hungarian botanists provide focal points among the plantings. In 1866 a small botanic garden devoted to public education rather than university study was founded in the park of Varosliget, Budapest. Four years later Count Sandór Vigyázó acquired the estate of Vacratot twenty miles north of Budapest, which is today the premier plant collection in Hungary. Vigyázó was an amateur natural scientist and together with leading garden designer Vilmos Jamber, who also worked for the Esterházy family, he created an arboretum, a botanic garden, greenhouses and a rock garden The latter contains more than 30.000 rocks collected by the people in villages from the surrounding countryside who were paid for each one they brought in. A labyrinth of natural streams flowing through the park was dammed to create an intricate network of water features ornamented with a traditional wooden watermill. On his death Vigyázó willed the garden to the Hungarian Academy of Science, which did not come into possession until 1946 due to a family contest of the will. In the meantime the manor house was demolished and replaced by the present pavilion in 1939. The park itself had been neglected for so long that it was not opened to the public until 1962. Among its present staff of thirty are scientists concerned with the conservation of the Hungarian flora and the study and

Horticultural University, Budapest

The university has inaugurated breeding programmes to provide improved ornamental plants for use by Hungary's landscape architects. It concentrates on the Rosaceae family and, in particular, on pyracantha, cotoneaster and sorbus cultivars.

149

Vacratot

The Hungarian Oak, Quercus frainetto, *a large fast-growing tree with fissured bark and lobed leaves.*

Opposite page:
In addition to its tree collection, Vacratot holds the largest collection of ornamental grasses in Central Europe.

introduction of plants from countries like North Korea and Cuba where on a recent expedition 150 tropical species new to science were discovered. During the period that Vigyázó was making the garden at Vacratot, Count Sándor Erdödy was pioneering the introduction of exotic trees on his estate at Vep. In 1890 Count Pál Bolza began the arboretum of Szarvas on the Great Hungarian Plain, which today holds over 1,600 taxa. A year later, near Szombathely, Count István Saághy started planting what has become one of the county's richest plant collections. After this burst of activity there was a lull until 1923. That year saw the foundation of the botanical garden of the University of Sopron, where the widely grown cultivar, *Chamaecyparis lawsoniana* 'Globosum' originated. Also at that time a sheltered arboretum overlooking Lake Balaton was begun by the Folly family, who still own it today. Its benign microclimate — the result of its south-facing, sheltered slope and the proximity of the lake — has enabled Mediterranean trees like the Italian cypress, *Cupressus sempervirens* and Spanish fir, *Abies pinsapo*, as well as the California coast redwood, *Sequoia sempervirens*, to flourish there.

Since 1945 a number of university botanic gardens have been established, the most noteworthy being that of the University of Horticulture and Food Sciences. It was started in the 1950s on the southern slopes of the Buda hills, which until the advent of phylloxera disease was one of the most productive wine-growing regions in central Europe. The garden of the former Institute of Viniculture forms the oldest part of the present garden, its outstanding trees including *Parrotia persica*, the hop hornbeam, *Ostrya carpinifolia* and three species of hackeberry, conveniently planted together to facilitate comparison. The entire campus now contains over 1,000 woody plant, 400 perennial and 200 bulb taxa. Sheltered niches between the centrally-heated buildings have provided opportunities for experimenting with tender plants, particularly broad-leaved evergreens, while there is also a concentration on hybrids of Hungarian origin. Hungary is the place where the natural distributions of the three European species of sorbus: *Sorbus aria*, *Sorbus aucuparia*, and *Sorbus torminalis*, meet and hybridize freely. From these many interesting selections have been made and are being tried.

Excluding arboreta and natural parks, there are now sixteen members of the Hungarian Committee of Botanical gardens — a fact which augurs well for the future of botany and horticulture in Hungary.

FROM BUDAPEST TO LAKE BALATON

The largest freshwater lake in Europe, Lake Balaton, is one of Hungary's most loved scenic areas. Its reed fringed shores wind in and out among forested hills. The peninsula of Tihany, crowned by a splendid Benedictine Monastery, can be seen from all points jutting out into the lake. The hills above Balatonfüred are a nature reserve of untouched woodland, animal and bird life. The lake shores have always been one of Hungary's favourite summer resorts.

The surrounding hills are dotted with villas and their luxuriant gardens in which all kinds of plants flourish because of the mildness of the lake-side climate. The main road between Budapest and Lake Balaton passes close to three outstanding English-style parks. Martonvásár, Alcsut and Deg date from the early eighteen hundreds while the park at Keszthely above Lake Balaton, was created at the end of the century. Martonvásár, the mansion of the Brunswick family, lies in the vicinity of Szekesfehervar in a marshy valley surrounded by wooded hills. The Brunswicks acquired the property in 1758 and constructed a Baroque house, church and formal garden over the next several years. In 1812, Count József Brunswick commissioned another family house at Dolna Krupa, now in Czechoslovakia, which was completed in 1818. So successful was the park that three years later Count Francis Brunswick com-

Martonvásár
The house as it appears in a mid nineteenth-century lithograph with the lake which was dug in order to drain the surrounding land. Note the deliberate contrast between the vertical lines of the Lombardy poplars and the rounded forms of the other trees. Courtesy of the Hungarian National Museum.

The swamp cypress, Taxodium distichum, *when grown near water, sends up «knees» of growth from the roots projecting above ground.*

A long timber bridge leads to an island in the lake where there is a plaque commemorating the Lombardy poplar under which Beethoven used to sit.

Martonvásár
The view across the lake showing the park as designed by C.H. Nebbien in 1821 and the house as reconstructed in neo-Gothic style in 1875.

Alcsut
The façade of the mansion designed by Mihály Pollack in 1818 is all that remains after World War II. It has now been stabilised to provide a focal point in the park. A weeping willow in Alcsut park contrasts in form and colour with the background trees and reflects perfectly in the dark green water.

missioned a similar park at Martonvásár. Responsible for both parks was the renowned landscape designer, Christian Heinrich Nebbien (1778-1841). A native of Lubeck, Nebbien travelled extensively over the course of his life, designing parks in Rumania, Czechoslovakia, Yugoslavia (all then part of Hungary), Bavaria, Austria and Poland.

At Martonvásár, Nebbien followed Repton's strategies very closely. The Szent Laszlo stream that flowed across the property was dammed to create a lake with an island very similar in shape and size to one which had been created earlier at Városliget. A wooden bridge connects the lawn that slopes gently down from the house to the island. A thatched icehouse and a classical viaduct were bounded with thick groves of indigenous trees varied with exotics such as silver limes, Lombardy poplars, tulip trees, Indian beans, purple beeches and weeping willows. Beethoven visited Martonvásár in 1800

Deg
A great English Oak, Quercus robur, *spreads its pendulous branches over the lawn in front of the house.*

and in 1806 and it is here that he composed his 'Appasionata' dedicated to the immortal loved one, Teresa van Brunswick's sister, Giuseppina. Part of the manor house is now a museum dedicated to the composer and in the theatre on the island a bust of Beethoven welcomes the guests. In 1870 the property was sold to the Dreher brewing family, who remodelled the house in the neo-Gothic style but left the park untouched. Martonvásár changed hands again in 1949 when it became the property of the Agricultural Research Institute of the Hungarian Academy of Sciences. The park is still in the possession of the institute and they have maintained it well, planting no fewer than 6,000 trees as recently as 1987.

The nearby and similar park of Alcsut was laid out for the Archduke József, the Empress Maria Theresia's grandson, and from 1796 until his death in 1847, the emperor's deputy or palatine in Hungary. As the royal palace in Buda did not have a garden, he created one on the 160 acre Margit Island in the Danube, below the castle. Since 1908 Margit Island has been a public park and each summer 100,000 annuals are planted in a colour scheme devised by the landscape architect Ildikó Kecskés. At Alcsut, from 1810 Archduke József, with the help of the court gardener Charles Tost and his own gardener, Rudolf Witsch, planted numerous trees including London plane, said to be the first in Hungary, oak, ash, beech, hornbeam and chestnut. Most remain today and have grown into outstanding specimens. In 1818 the archduke commissioned a house for Alcsut from Mihály Pollak (1773-1855). Viennese

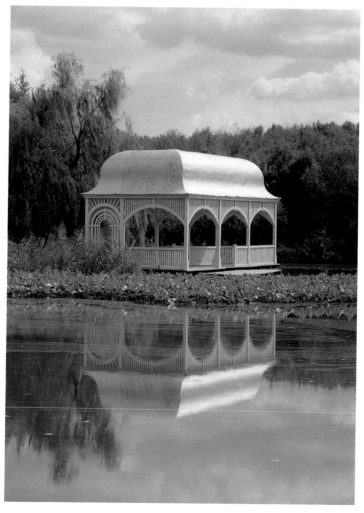

A lawn slopes from the portico of the house designed by Mihály Pollack c. 1821 to a lake formed out of a group of meandering streams.

A lakeside kiosk of painted trelliswork in Turkish style embellishes an island.

Kesthely

The mansion as reconstructed in 1883-87 by the Viennese architect, Viktor Rumpelmeyer, was set in a garden laid out by E.H. Milner, the English assistant of Sir Joseph Paxton.

by birth but Hungarian by adoption, both Mihály and his brother Leopoldo were among the leading neo-Classical architects of the day. Although most of this house was destroyed during World War II, the front façade survived and was ingeniously stabilized so that, together with a nearby orangery, it now forms an architectural focal point in the park. The park's design followed Repton's recommendations closely. As at Martonvásár, an artificial lake was formed by damming a stream, sloping lawns were laid out to alternate with dense groves of trees, and discreetly positioned paths were laid out which crossed over streams by means of stone or wooden bridges. The archduke took particular care with the tree planting and as a result there are now excellent specimens of Austrian pine, ironwood, white and black maple, purple beech, Turkish hazel, Japanese acacia, elm, poplar and the outstanding cedar of Lebanon planted in 1820.

The third of the trio of early-nineteenth-century parks at Deges, south of Alcsut, now a school, was originally owned by the

A pair of stone lions decorate the façade of a neo-classical well-house in the park.

159

Lake Héviz
Tropical waterlilies flower from May to October in the lake water issuing from the hot springs of one of Hungary's oldest spas. The breeding of waterlilies resulted in a race of hybrids which transformed European watergardening in the late nineteenth century.

Festetics family and like Alcsut with a house designed by Mihály Pollak. Its porticoed front looks down over long, sloping lawns to a lake formed out of a group of meandering streams covered with various kinds of water lily. Across one, an iron bridge leads to an island with a kiosk in the Turkish style and a two-storey Dutch-style house built in 1870 and now a museum. Limes, maples, poplars and weeping willows overhang the streams and a massive common oak extends its broad, feathered limbs over the lawn at the back of the house. The Festetics were also associated with Keszthely, the fourth and final park in the area, which lies on the western tip of Lake Balaton. Count György Festetics (1755-1819), noted for his enthusiasm for classical ideals, founded Europe's first agricultural academy, known as the Georgikon, at Keszthely, along with a public library known as the Helikon. The garden itself was not begun until the 1880s, when Tassilo Festetics married the daughter of the Scottish Duke of Hamilton. He commissioned the architect Rumpelmeyer to enlarge the house and the English garden designer Henry Ernest Milner (1819-1894) to redesign the 180-acre park and garden in 1886. Milner was assistant to Sir Joseph Paxton, premier garden designer of Victorian England, and his practice was initially confined to the north of England around the Duke of Devonshire's estate at Chatsworth. Later it became an impressively international one, and in addition to Hungary, his obituary in the *Gardener's Chronicle* mentioned his work in Ireland, Belgium, France, the Rhineland, Sweden and Denmark. Milner's habit was to provide a formal garden, often semi-circular in shape, near the house, which gradually gave way to flowing lines of shrubberies and broad views of distant parkland. The garden at Keszthely takes this form. The parkland itself is given variety through the imposition of artificial mounds

Kormend

The house and garden of the Batthyany family were designed by the outstanding Italian master Donato Felice de Allio between 1730 and 1745. In 1799 and 1810 the eastern part of the garden was converted into an informal landscape park, creating a lake with exotic trees and reached by timber bridges. The lake was the result of the diversion and regulation of the river Raba.

161

and hollows that create a pleasantly-undulating surface, a practice
that Milner learned from Paxton, who first used it in the arboretum at Derby. Milner also lowered a road to open the view from
the house to the lake and planted a sunken garden with dwarf
conifers, a rocky fernery, a rhododendron and laurel shrubberies.
Beyond Keszthely and a magnificent grove of eucalyptus, lies
lies Lake Héviz, one of the oldest spas in Hungary and yet

another of Count György's creations. Radioactive, the water of the lake never goes below thirty degrees. Héviz is of interest to gardeners because of the unique collection of red tropical water lilies that flower there from April to October thanks to the artificial climate created by its hot springs. White water lilies grow spontaneously in the nearby canals.

Fenekpuzsta
The Festetics stud farm from an 1884 painting by Emil Adam.

TATA, GEOLOGICAL PARK

The vigorously-serpentine paths of white gravel contrast effectively with the green grass. The lawn surfaces are broken by island beds of mixed planting and carefully arranged groups of quarried stones.

Tata

Uncut or rough-cut stones quarried on the site of this geological demonstration garden are decorated with linear, cuneiform script to remind the visitor of the ancient habitation of the area.

Opposite page:
Natural rock faces have been exposed and seized upon as opportunities to do some natural rock gardening.

Situated between the Vertes and Gerecse hills, the town of Tata is well known for its scenic lakes and canals and its impressive eighteenth-century Baroque architecture. The park of the Esterházy family in the town of Tata was enhanced by the ruins of a fifteenth-century castle, a Turkish tent and an artificial ruin by Charles de Moreau, the Viennese architect who also created the Esterházy family's English park at Kismarton in 1805. But Tata's most distinctive feature today is the series of excavated prehistoric settlements and geological viewing areas scattered across it. The Tata geological conservation area is found at the base of Calvary Hill and has been designed to educate the general public about Hungary's geological history. Despite the emphasis placed on ancient history, the park is landscaped as a geological demonstration as well as a garden.

The Jurassic and Cretaceous periods (195 to 65 million years ago) are well represented by formations of white Dachstein limestone as old as 235 million years. Later formations of clay, gravel, sand and travertine stretch beneath the nearby Old Lake and can be seen along its banks. When the Dachstein limestone was laid down, the earth's atmosphere was still

so heavy with carbon dioxide that only extremely primitive club-mosses were able to survive. When the subsequent clays were deposited — 35-1.5 million years ago — Hungary enjoyed a sub-tropical climate and supported a vegetation similar to that of South-East Asia today.

The walk through the garden begins at the top of Calvary Hill where a relatively complete Jurassic sequence — 140 feet high — of limestone rock has been unearthed. This rock was laid down in a time when the Mediterranean sea still covered the area, and fossil remains of tidal organisms are clearly visible within it. Evidence of a much later point in prehistory can also be seen here: the limestone fissures once served as shelter for prehistoric flint-mining man.

The walk continues through an area of limestone formations from the Cretaceous period. Tata Castle and many of the houses of the town are largely constructed from this Limestone. The Cretaceous period was a very long chapter in the earth's evolutionary history. It saw, among other things, the development of trees as we know them today from the more primitive tree ferns that previously had covered the world for millions of years. During this period much of the area that today is Tata, was an island in the inland Mediterranean area, and the limestone here and there shows the effects of wave action against what was once a rocky shore. The walk ends on a fault-plane in the limestone.

Several quarried stones have been arranged in abstract sculptural groups and serve as focal points for a number of plant groups typically grown on limestone soils. Both in its untouched natural state and as an object of human creation, the imposing beauty of limestone is everywhere in evidence.

YUGOSLAVIA

The Mediterranean country of Yugoslavia is a world of its own, a microcosm combining Eastern and Western, Turkish and European, Islamic and Christian influences. A dozen different ethnic groups are divided into six constituent republics — Slovenia, Croatia, Serbia, Bosnia-Hercegovina, Montenegro and Macedonia with two different autonomous provinces, Vojvodina and Kosovo. Large expanses of virgin Mediterranean forest, rapidly disappearing through development in other countries, survive along Yugoslavia's Adriatic coast, most notably on the island of Mljet. In the mountains of the interior, a typical Central European forest of mixed deciduous and coniferous species thrives. The stands of beech, silver fir and common spruce in the virgin forest of Peručica in Bosnia are considered the best in Europe. In the twenty national park areas, a wide variety of native and endemic species can be enjoyed including the beautifully conical Serbian spruce, *Picea omorika*, which grows among limestone rocks above the river Drina. The Bosnian pine, *Pinus leucodermis*, the *Quercus trojana* are but some of the native trees to be seen here in their typical natural locations.

The Romans occupied the Northern Dalmatian coast as early as 200 BC. Their civilization gradually spread inland until it covered most of the present-day Yugoslavia. Yet today only fragments of their gardens remain, such as the terraces and fishponds at Veriga Bay on the Brioni island or at Stobi in Southern Macedonia. Even within the monumental seaside villa of the Emperor Diocletian at Split, all traces of the Roman garden that once lay there have been obliterated by later development.

During the period when Byzantium was the centre of the Roman Empire, gardens were laid out in Yugoslavia around royal residences, monasteries and in the towns. Excavations at the early sixth-century town of Caričin Grad in Serbia have shown how gardens were integrated with the building complexes. Of the later gardens in the fortified Orthodox monasteries little remains except written descriptions. Some sense of their atmosphere can be obtained, however, by visiting Serbian monasteries like Mileśeva, Studenica and Žiča with their stewponds, strawberry beds, beehive-filled orchards, flower gardens with roses and Madonna lillies, and crown imperials flowering under quince trees.

The Turkish invasion in the fourteenth century marked the beginning of five centuries of Islamic presence in the southern parts of the country. Islam brought with it an opulent architectural and horticultural style that manifested itself in the arrangement of the mosques, residences and their attendant courtyards. While there are few historic residential gardens left, a general impression of their character can be obtained by walking through the Turkish quarters of cities such as Sarajevo where luxuriant gardens still form a part of the domestic tradition. One can also visit the many houses of the Turkish pashas (military governors) which have been turned into museums. Of the flowers to be found here most interesting are the many forms of damask roses not cultivated in Western Europe. The most frequently planted of these is the 'Sugar' rose, so called because of the delicious jam made from its petals. Good examples of courtyards with fountains, ornamental pavings and plantings can still be seen in the mosques of places like Sarajevo and Mostar. In addition some Muslim cemeteries will attract the attention of landscape architects. The most notable of these is that of Ali Fakovak at Sarajevo with its dominant position and beautifully-designed tombstones layed out in an intriguing spiral design.

The city-state of Ragusa, (now called Dubrovnik), retained its independence from the Turks by forging alliances with Venice and other Italian city-states on the other side of the Adriatic sea. The faith of its citizens remained Catholic rather than Orthodox, and expressed itself in the impressive Dominican and Franciscan monasteries in the city. The design of their cloister gardens is similar to that in the monasteries of the Western Mediterranean, particularly those in Spain. Their present planting, however, reflects a late nineteenth-century scheme of interest for its old-fashioned rose cultivars of a kind now rarely seen in Western Europe. Rose 'La France', one of the first hybrid tea roses bred in France in 1867 and rose 'Paul Neyron', a hybrid perpetual also bred there in 1869, are good examples. Renaissance humanism also spread to Dubrovnik, and was expressed in the conception of villa life as the ideal environment for the enhancement of man through the practice and enjoyment of the arts and sciences. In pursuit of these ideals, the patricians of Ragusa built a series of villas along the coast both north and south of the city. Many remain, though in widely varying states of conservation, and provide a unique opportunity for the garden historian to study the early Renaissance villa and its garden.

The Turkish advance was stopped in 1699. There followed a period of relative peace and prosperity during which the influence of the Grand Baroque style of gardening infiltrated those parts of the country which were then under the dominance of the Austro-Hungarian Empire. Slovenia, and later Croatia and Vojvodina, all had examples of gardens of this kind of which only those of Dornava near Ptuj in Slovenia

survive. At the beginning of the eighteenth century, at Dornava, the Attems family converted a fourteenth-century manor house into the present palace with its formal garden. An entrance avenue over a mile long begins with a sculpted figure on a pedestal and ends in a forecourt in front of the house. On the garden front, the axis is continued in another courtyard, a parterre around a central figure of Neptune and a formally-planted orchard which replaces in this case the formal woodland of forest trees more typical of the Baroque garden. The entire garden was originally decorated with a rich collection of sculpture, the majority of which remains.

The landscape of the northern regions of Slovenia, Croatia and Vojvodina, which together constitute the southern extension of the Great Hungarian Plain, is largely flat. In contrast to the more mountainous regions of the south, it is ideally suited to the creation of large-scale landscape layouts, be they of the formal Baroque or later informal landscape style. During the years when the area was part of the Austro-Hungarian Empire, Slovenia was annexed to Austria but Croatia formed part of Hungary. It was thus that the landscape park was introduced to Yugoslavia from Hungary, the first notable parks in the style being designed by the German-born but Hungarian-based landscape gardener Christian Heinrich Nebbien (1778-1841). The recent discovery of his extensive body of correspondence in the National Library at Bratislava in Czechoslovakia allows us to identify and date his work in Yugoslavia. In an article of 1818 he refers to a project carried out for a park at Elemir, and in another essay of 1821 he describes the two parks he created in Vojvodina: one of St Gyorgy at Zitište for Anton Kis de Iterbe and the other at Ecka for August Lazar de Etske. Both are south of the present-day city of Zrenjamin.

Hungarian influence continued with Bishop Haulik of Zagreb, a man of Hungarian origin who created the first public park in South-East Europe. The 450-acre Maksimir Park on the outskirts of Zagreb had been given a formal layout by Bishop Vrhovac at the end of the seventeenth century. In 1846, Haulik felled much of the park woodland to provide the open meadows and lakes which are a conspicuous feature of its layout today. A straight avenue leads from the entrance gate to a central kiosk raised on a mound. From here four different views open out upon tree-lined glades and across artificial lakes to the park's edges. In 1850 the scheme was illustrated by the lithographer Johann Zaschke to accompany a description of the park published by the Bishop. Sadly the great clarity and simplicity of this design was later diminished by the addition of a zoo.

Two Croatian landscape parks which can be visited today are Opeka near Varaždim and Našice (now in Vojvodina).

Although the date over the entrance gate at Opeka is 1674, the 160-acre park was planted by Count Bombelles in the mid-nineteenth century to become the largest tree collection in Croatia. It still boasts good specimens of weeping spruce, swamp cypress, nettle, lime and tulip trees which grow among old groves of hardy hybrid rhododendrons. The medieval fortress at Nasice was altered by Count Pejačević in the neo-Classical style at the beginning of the nineteenth century, its park and lake were only created in the second half of the century by clearing the surrounding beech and whitebeam woods. Both parks borrow from the surrounding landscape to augment their effect. At Opeka, the tree-lined glades guide the eye to the distant wooded hills while at Našice they are so extensive as to echo in the mind's eye the seemingly limitless surrounding plain.

In time two separate conceptions of what defined a landscape park began to develop, in the first a formal garden was reintroduced around a house in order to link it with surrounding parkland, while in the second a great variety of exotic trees were added to woodland plantings to create what were, in effect, arboreta. An example of the first direction is Hajdučica, in the Banat on the Rumanian border which has formal gardens with pools and a maze immediately surrounding a house dating from the 1880s. Volcjipotok, near Llubljana, has an Italianate terrace garden linking the house to its parkland. The best examples of the second direction survive in two contrasting parks in Slovenia — Viltos Castle near Maribor with its inland continental climate, and Nova Gorica on the northern Adriatic coast, with its milder Mediterranean climate. Vilto's collection of hardy trees contains many American species such as the Kentucky Coffee Tree, *Gymnocladus dioica* and the large-leaved *Magnolia macrophylla* as well as Japanese species like the Umbrella Pine, *Sciadopitys verticillata*. Nova Gorica's collection, in the eight-acre park and its neo-Moorish palace, contains good specimens of the Cork oak, *Quercus suber*, the Bhutan cypress, *Cupressus torulosa*, the Camphor tree, *Cinnamonum camphora*, and many old camellia hybrids.

The development of seaside resorts along the Adriatic coast in the late nineteenth and early twentieth century led to a proliferation of villas along with their attendant gardens. The eclectic and sometimes fantastic architectural styles in which they were built are matched by an equal eclecticism in the design and planting of their gardens, which were full of 'subtropical' vegetation in that mixture of palms, eucalyptus, cactus, agave and citrus fruits familiar from all Mediterranean gardens of the period. Many of these villa gardens are now overgrown and the villas themselves ruined or sub-divided into apartments. Visually the resort town of Opatija remains Austrian *fin-de-siècle* in flavour. It was founded in 1844 when Iginio Scarpa, a local businessman, built the Villa Angiolina, the beautiful park of which is still maintained and open to the public. Giant coast redwoods, eucalyptus and laurel magnolias as well as Lebanon, Atlas and Deodar cedars dominate while camellias, forsythias, crepe myrtles, tamarisk and bougainvillea contribute their colour; palms, agaves and bananas their sculptural form and citrus trees their fruit according to season. In 1845, King Frederick August II of Saxony made a botanical exploration of the rich natural flora of the area. Later it became a favourite watering place of the Austrian emperors and their courts. The villa gardens, the most outstanding of which is at the Villa Frappart, by the architect Carl Seidl, make a fascinating study in *fin-de-siècle* planting and design.

The collapse of the Austro-Hungarian Empire after World War I and the creation of the new state of Yugoslavia led to a re-evaluation of gardening styles and the evolution of a new, restrained approach to complement modern styles of architecture. An excellent example of this approach is the villa and garden that the sculptor Ivan Meštrović (1883-1962) designed for himself on a site west of Split in 1937. The villa is a long low building of dazzling white Brač limestone in a style which is a mixture of modernism and eclecticism. Next to it are formal gardens designed by Meštrović as a setting for his sculpture. During this same period, the conservative Prince Paul of Yugoslavia, then regent of the new state, chose a Florence-based English designer, Cecil Pinsent, to design an architectural ornament in a neo-Baroque style for the garden of his summer residence in the mountains at Brdo near Kranj in Slovenia.

Though new botanic gardens and arboreta have been founded in the post World War II period, the most remarkable recent development has been the creation of a national park system that boasts some of the most outstanding natural conservation areas in Central or Eastern Europe, many of them managed in an exemplary way. The Plitvice National Park in Croatia and the National Park of Sutješka in Montenegro are notable examples of the contribution which landscape design can make towards opening areas of outstanding natural beauty and scientific interest to the public without spoiling them.

Climatic and topographical diversity combined with a rich mixture of historical and cultural influence make Yugoslavia a country of great interest for the botanist, horticulturalist and garden historian alike.

VILLAS OF THE DUBROVNIK RENAISSANCE

The most complete example of a villa and garden complex of the Dubrovnik Renaissance to survive. Steps lead to the first floor roof terrace.

Trees shade the large water tank to reduce surface evaporation in summer and to keep the fish cool in its shallow waters.

Villa Sorkočević
The rising sun penetrates the vaulted interior of the loggia, throwing the spirally-fluted columns into sharp relief.

Opposite page:
A cool lavabo conveniently located by the house entrance and also by the steps to the first floor terrace.

After the Turkish invasion of the Balkan peninsula and the subsequent capture of most of Eastern and Southern Yugoslavia, Dubrovnik (then known as Ragusa) was able to remain as an independent city-state by contrasting political alliances with Venice and the other side of the Adriatic sea. Along with these political links went cultural ties, the Italian Renaissance in the arts and sciences being paralleled by a similar renaissance in Dubrovnik. Poets wrote love poems and epic cycles in both Latin and Serbo-Croatian. Newly composed comedies and pastoral dramas were performed. Learned treaties were published on subjects such as astronomy, mathematics and natural history. One native of the city, Jurac Dragišić, went to Florence where he became tutor to the sons of Lorenzo de' Medici and, later, defending counsel for the neo-Platonist philosopher Pico della Mirandola during his trial by the Inquisition.

Dubrovnik also began to enjoy extensive wealth as it became the refuge for many noble families from Turkish occupied parts of the country and as its businessmen gradually built up lucrative trading positions between the Turkish Empire and the rest of the Mediterranean world. Its Republican Constitution, like that of Venice, was strictly aristocratic and it was the city's powerful nobles who built the unique series of early Renaissance seaside villas and garden features in this chapter. As only isolated examples of seaside villas, from either the classical Roman or Italian Renaissance periods survive, the Dubrovnik group presents the garden historian with an unequalled opportunity to study the villas of the early Renaissance period. This is particularly the case as none of them were affected by series of earthquakes which so severely damaged the city itself during the seventeenth century.

As early as 1440, the native chronicler Philip de Diversis noted that the city benefited from 'numerous vineyards in the surrounding area, monumental palaces and wonderful gardens'. The gardens from the following century were usually surrounded by high walls crowned with decorative rather than functional battlements. Their villas were assymetrical in design, often L-shaped — with one wing a two-storeyed residence, the other a one-storeyed combination of storage, water cistern and boathouse with a rooftop terrace. These terraces were often adorned with a covered pavilion and stone benches overlooking the sea, and could be reached from the first-floor loggia of the main house. Thus house and garden, interior and exterior were intimately connected. The gardens themselves were formal, with terraces, pergolas and geometrically-planned planting beds. The scarcity of available water demanded that small fountains or irrigation channels and tanks take the place of their more spectacular counterparts in Western Europe. In a handful of gardens, larger fishponds

were joined to the sea by canals. Enclosed by high walls, these ponds had a powerful visual effect introducing the space and energy of the sea into the circumscribed garden environment.

The earliest of these gardens, still in existence date from 1520, as does the part-Gothic, part-Renaissance villa of the Sorkočević family at Lapad in the Western suburbs of the city. Its garden, only 3,000 square yards in size, was not completed until the second half of the century and is the best preserved of the period. Vaulted Renaissance-style arcades surround on three sides a terrace overlooking the sea. In the centre is a fishpond surrounded by flower beds in a formal plan and divided by vine-shaded, pergola-covered paths; a flight of steps rises from the garden to a roof terrace. On the landward side of the villa, a pair of further wings frames a formal flower garden from which another staircase leads to a first-floor loggia. The villa's creator, whose escutcheon is carved in stone over all its gates and cisterns, was the noted humanist, Petar Sorkočević. He was assisted in its design by the architect Silvio Antunovic from the island of Korčula and the sculptor, Petar Petrovic.

Another late sixteenth-century garden of the Sorkočević family survives at the head of the long sea-creek of Riječka Dubrovačka north of the city. The formal parterre with its walks, cross-walks and carved stone pergolas are still visible as is the monumental flight of stone steps leading directly down to the sea. On the north shore of the creek — once a favourite resort of the Ragusa nobility but now very builtup — stand the remains of the sixteenth-century Sorgo-Gučetić villa, including a monumental staircase decorated with stone baskets. The Sorkočević villas are paralleled by a pair once owned by the Skorbibuha family on the island of Sirpon, the largest of the Elaphite islands north of Dubrovnik. The villas have an interesting terraced articulation and richly-carved pergola pillars. The town of Gruž, now the busy main harbour for Dubrovnik, also retains, hidden behind high walls, a series of sixteenth-century summer villas with arcaded loggias, boathouses, water cisterns and rooftop pavilions, all in small parks. While none of these gardens is complete today, enough of each remains to enable a visitor to build up a complete picture of the design and planting of a sixteenth-century seaside villa — an opportunity to be found nowhere else in the Mediterranean.

THE CLOISTER GARDENS
OF DUBROVNIK

The Franciscan Convent

The seat-lined promenade of the cloister garden evokes the social nature of life under the Franciscan rule. The stilted arches of the arcade are in a Veneto-Byzantine style.

Opposite page:
Circular openings let high-level light into the recesses of the cloister walk.
The original planting of orange trees in the cloister garden has been replaced by a late nineteenth-century romantic planting of flowering shrubs and sub-tropical foliage plants.

The cloister gardens of the Dominican and Franciscan monasteries in Dubrovnik are among the few Eastern European gardens of the medieval period to maintain a semblance of their original design.

The medieval cloister garden evolved from the peristyle or colonnaded courtyard of the Roman country villa. The most obvious design difference between the two is in the placement of their columns. Those surrounding the cloister gardens do not reach the ground as do those which surround the Roman courtyards or Arab patios for that matter, but rather rest on dwarf walls of about sitting height. The traditional belief that cloister plantings were arranged in formal beds has recently been questioned by garden historians and for the moment it is a matter that must remain open to debate. However there is no disputing the fact that different orders evolved designs to suit the requirements of their own particular monastic rules. The Benedictine order for example, had a standard plan of cross-paths meeting around a central fountain. The Cistercensian order, by contrast, developed a fountain in the form of a lavabo which was placed in a corner of the cloister near the refectory so that the monks could wash before eating. The Franciscan order used a variety of plans, one of the most noteworthy having a wide central walk lined with stone benches leading to an ornamental well at one end. This plan reflects the more social way of life of the Franciscan monastic rule in that it allowed for the evening promenade. The monks could exercise on the promenade and relax on the seats and discuss the day's events.

The monastery of the Franciscan nuns at Pedralbes near Barcelona has the best known such plan, but the Franciscan monastery in Dubrovnik has one of equal interest. Built in 1317 inside the western gate of the city, to the design of the Montenegrin architect, Mihoje Brajkov (d.1335), the cloister has an arcade which is supported by the most elegant twin columns with carved capitals in a transitional Romanesque-Gothic style. At intervals in the wall above, circular openings let high-level light into the shadowy recesses of the cloister below. Over a hundred years later, in 1435, Ralko Brajković added a pierced-stone balustrade above the cloister. This impressive structure is decorated with fantastic carved beasts, monsters and mythological creatures in the best romanesque tradition. The present garden is planted in the late nineteenth-century sub-tropical style featuring a random mixture of trees with sculptural forms like fan palms and cordylines and with a lower tier of flowering shrubs. Cloister gardens paved and planted solely with orange trees are almost always found in Southern Europe. This type of design appears to have first been used in the courtyards of the twelfth-century mosques (now cathedrals) of Cordoba and Seville in Spain. The orange trees are planted in intervals corresponding to the columns in the cloister while the individual trees are linked by narrow irrigation channels sunk into the surrounding paving. Similar but more modest designs can be found in the Palacio de la Diputación in Barcelona and in the Convent of Christ, at Tomar, Portugal. Another, however, can be found in the Dominican monastery inside the eastern gate of the city of Dubrovnik. Built in a graceful late Gothic style to the modified designs of Maso di Bartolomeo (1406-1456) of Florence, the garden is planted with orange trees around a central, Venetian well-head of 1559. The latter has a later renaissance overthrow erected in 1623.

TRSTENO

The view from the house to the island of Lopud is broken by the contrasting forms of a Chinese fan palm and a Mediterranean cypress. The recently restored Baroque fountain, depicting Neptune.

'I give praise for my neighbours, for water, for a healthy climate and for the work of a noble landlord. Here traveller, you see the visual traces of the human race, where man's skillful art has improved wild nature'. So runs a 1502 inscription in Latin on a stone tablet in the garden of Trsteno, the estate founded and developed by the Gučetić family over 450 years until it was willed in 1948 by the last Count Gucetić to the Yugoslav Academy of Science and Art.

The Gučetić (in Italian, Gozze) family gave Dubrovnik a number of outstanding personalities — princes, ambassadors, poets and writers — who advanced its interests and carried its fame throughout Europe. One of them, the poet Nikola Viktor Gučetić (1549-1610), is particularly associated with Trsteno, but all retained their attachment to the place where the family originated, perhaps as far back as the eighth century. Although set in a harsh limestone landscape, Trsteno is watered by a

Trsteno
Plants of architectural form from different climates are brought into unusual conjunction: these yuccas, from a dry-zone American climate have as a background Chusan palms from a wet-zone Chinese climate, the latter flourishing on account of the garden's natural spring.

Now owned by the Yugoslav Academy of Science and Art, the park is used as an acclimatisation centre and nursery for the test introduction of ornamental plants.

spring which has been harnessed and distributed by means of aqueducts to every part of the estate so that the property forms a green oasis in the midst of a virtually treeless landscape. The late fifteenth-century house is surprisingly modest in conception and size, each of its two floors having a standard plan of two bedrooms leading off either end of a central hall or reception rooms. This layout was so common for a Dalmatian nobleman's house that the Venetians in those days had a rhyme about it:

> *Quatro stanze, un salon*
> *Ze la casa d'un Schiavon.*
> (Four rooms, one salon,
> that's the house of a Slav.)

The house is equally modest externally. Set on a platform overlooking the sea, its dressed limestone façades harmonize with the rugged limestone mountains behind. A carved escutcheon and votive shrine are the only decoration. However because it functioned as a summer villa in which much of the day's activities took place out of doors, the gardens and immediate surroundings of the house are laid out on a comparatively elaborate geometric plan. Opposite the entrance door is a formal walk covered with a pergola and leading to a belvedere overlooking the sea and the island of Lopud, which is separated from the mainland by the narrow Kolocepski channel. The pergola is in a transitional Gothic-Renaissance style that gives a fascinating demonstration of how that still ubiquitous garden feature, the pergola, evolved from the medieval cloister walk. Elements of the latter — thin octagonal columns with primitively-formed but exquisitely-carved caps and bases resting on dwarf walls — are here used to form a free-standing garden walk covered with shade-giving timber lattice.

The walk widens at one point to form a miniature, tree-shaded *piazza* surrounded by stone seats and overlooking the sea and the setting sun ideal for the evening intercourse. The dwarf walls and the seats are used in summer as a platform on which to display a medley of potted plants while the entire area is shaded by the leathery fronds of the Chinese fan-palm, *Trachycarpus fortunei*. The parterre on either side of the centre walk has a formal design of stone-edged beds around a Baroque fountain depicting Neptune attended by sea-nymphs which was erected in 1736. However, the geometry has been all but obscured by exuberant planting. Fruit trees — loquats, figs, peaches and citrus in variety — contributes an air of abundance while dwarf palms — sago and European palms, dasylirions and cordylines — add their bold architectural foliage. Banksian and China roses, oleander and bougainvillea add the brilliance of their summer flowering. Architectural and sculptural focal points - aqueducts, stone and earthenware pots and the small oratory of St Jeronim — emerge from the vegetation.

A natural spring, harnessed and distributed by means of an aqueduct throughout the estate, has enabled the formation of a green oasis in the midst of a harsh limestone landscape.

Trsteno

An ambiguity of scale results from the setting of this amphora against an apparently limitless sea and sky.

Around the five-acre garden dating from the sixteenth century, a larger park extends over a steep hillside that has been carved into no fewer than 462 terraces. Its skyline is dominated by the solid green spires of hundreds of Italian cypresses rising above a waving sea of lower foliage — Aleppo pine, oriental hornbeam and black locust. In early spring the woods light up with flowering wild cherry, *Prunus avium*. Later they are brightened by the flowers of hundreds of Manna ash. An understorey of evergreen bay laurel, laurestinus, myrtle and arbutus give cool shade to the drives and walks. Avenues of Fortune's palm and Golden bamboo add an exotic note. Along the open, sunny terraces of the outer reaches of the park, silvery olives are undercarpeted with a Mediterranean *garrigue* of kermes, oak, gorse, thyme, lavender and rosemary with an occasional sculptural form of agave, yucca or prickly pear. The tree collection numbers over three hundred species and cultivars. The imperial paulownia, the paper mulberry, the camphor tree and various eucalyptus grow among a good collection of conifers including the Japanese cedar, the Himalayan cypress, the Chinese fir, the maidenhair tree and the Chinese Plum Yew. When the park was taken over by the Academy of Science and Art it became an acclimatisation centre.

The cypress, symbolizing permanence, and the flowering tree, symbolizing transience, have been contrasted for centuries in Middle Eastern and Mediterranean gardens.

THE POET'S GARDEN,
in the Island of Hvar

Hektorović Villa
The villa complex of the poet with its original tower, adjoining house, garden, fishpond and dovecote remains remarkably complete.

A blind arcade with stilted arches in the Veneto-Byzantine style spans the holes and perches of the garden's dovecote.

A cycad, from a plant family of great antiquity, grows in a terracotta twin-handled urn.

Cosimo de' Medici, the ruler of Renaissance Florence, wrote in one of his last letters: 'Yesterday, I came to the villa of Careggi not to cultivate my fields but my soul'. The ideal of the country villa as an environment in which both to study and compose literary and philosophical works was central to the world of renaissance humanism. It is an idea which re-occurs throughout history. The Roman writer Pliny (61-112), built a pair of contrasting country villas. In China the connection between the literary life and gardening already was being exemplified in the fifth century by Hsieh Ling-yun and T'ao Ch'ien, two masters of Chinese poetry who were also accomplished gardeners. In eighteenth-century England, Alexander Pope, created a garden deliberately intended for retirement and contemplation at Twickenham, near London. In early nineteenth-century Germany, Goethe made a garden at Weimar. So too did the Yugoslavian Hanibal Jucić (1485-1553) and Petar Hektorović (1487-1572), both of whom created gardens on the island of Hvar.

Hvar is the fourth largest island in the Adriatic Sea. It came under Venetian rule at the beginning of the fifteenth century, after which it prospered as a producer of wine, olives, figs and honey and also as the principal seaport between Venice and her chief colony Crete. In the sixteenth and seventeenth centuries, Hvar was also noted as a town devoted to literature and the theatre and produced a number of writers, poets, historians and diplomats. Chief among these were Jucić, author of *Robinje* (*The Slave-girl*), the first non-religious drama in Croatian, and Hektorović, whose pastoral dialogue on the subject of fishing exerted a considerable literary influence. Both poets had a house in the town of Hvar. The comparatively modest house of Hektorović is built into the town wall in a street of patrician houses, while on a higher level stands the mansion of Jucić, now a Benedictine convent. Both poets also had country villas on the island. Jucić's is situated close to town on a road which departs from behind the cathedral to the neighbouring village of Milna. Set against a backdrop of hills covered with pinewoods, olive groves and fields of lavender and rosemary, the garden retains its sixteenth-century outline and its well-head, carved in the Venetian manner with the Jucić and Gazaravić coats-of-arms. It is now planted as a botanical garden which demonstrates to advantage Hvar's favourable climate. It has the highest number of sunshine

Hektorović Villa

An arcade surrounds and shades the fishpool in which, according to local lore, the weather can be forecast by watching the direction in which the fish swim. Tablets with inscriptions are set into the walls.

A light iron-and-wire framework supports vines which shade the garden path.

Opposite page:
Octagonal columns, with broad caps and bases in the Veneto-Byzantine style, support pergolas which act as the major space-divisions within the garden.

hours in the Adriatic and is often compared in this respect with Madeira.

Hektorović's country villa is situated in the tiny town of Stari Grad which served as the island's capital until it was superseded by Hvar in the twelfth century. Stari Grad is picturesquely situated at the end of a five mile long fjord and the villa itself, known as Tvrdalj and built around 1520, is situated in a small waterfront square. Its garden is developed around a courtyard with a central fishpond surrounded and shaded by a vaulted arcade. Fishponds played an integral part in the design of medieval and early Renaissance gardens. Both ornamental fish such as carp, and edible species such as perch, bream, tench and pike were housed in its waters. 'Lazy' fish species which do not require much excercise were favoured in small ponds such as this, and the different species were often separated by underwater nets. If it was not possible to excavate a deep pool, because of underlying rock, shade was provided by high surrounding walls or arcades as in this case. The pool sides are embellished with bas-relief carvings and inscriptions, such as are found in many poets' gardens, designed to have a direct effect on emotions. There is also a dovecote and a 'sparrowcote'. Dovecotes were an indispensable adjunct of country villas of the time and they provided not only food for the table but sound and elegant movement for the garden. The dovecote in Tvrdalj is of the typical gable form with holes and perches provided under the roof. The 'sparrowcote' however is an exceptional feature and shows to good effect the whimsical intentions of the garden's creator. The principal interest of both this and the Jucic garden is the way in which they fit into that worldwide and historical phenomenon — the poet's garden.

LLUBLJANA ARBORETUM, PUBLIC PARKS AND BOTANIC GARDENS

In the nineteenth century increasing urbanization led to the establishment of public parks or gardens in towns and cities throughout Europe. The urban population's need for exercise and fresh air was matched by a wide spread recognition of the desirability of public education and the improvement in matters of horticulture generally. The building of educational displays, monuments and busts of national heroes was also seen as a good opportunity for reminding the citizenry of the great feats of their country's past. The first botanic garden in Yugoslavia was founded at Llubljana, capital of Slovenia, in 1810. Its six-acre garden today boasts the second largest plant collection in the country with over 4,500 plant taxa and its staff are making a special study of Slovenian flora. The first public park, Maksimir Park, was founded in Zagreb in 1846.

Throughout Europe in the late nineteenth century, obsolete fortifications with which many cities were encumbered were converted into city parks. In Italy, for example, the city of Lucca is surrounded by a park that follows the line of the old city walls. In Portugal, the principal city park lies atop the old fortress of St George. So in Belgrade, the Kalemegdan Park was laid out over the remains of the city's hilltop fortress, once one of the largest in existence. From its heights it offers Belgrade's citizenry magnificent views over the Danube and its fertile plain which stretches for hundreds of miles up into Central Europe. Many cities also gained public parks through the conversion of former royal palace gardens. The Topčider Park in Belgrade, for example, surrounds the former palace of Prince Miloš Obrenović, who wrested Serbian autonomy from the Ottoman Empire in 1830. In the same period regional capitals like Zagreb and Llubljana also acquired extensive and still excellently-maintained public parks. So also did smaller towns, most notably Tivat in Montenegro and Gorica on Lake Ohrid in Macedonia.

Yugoslavia's second botanic garden was founded in Belgrade in 1874 and its third in Zagreb in 1889. Each is about thirteen acres in area. Belgrade has a collection of approximately 2,000 taxa today whereas Zagreb boasts around 10,000. An intensive period of activity began in the period after World

Volcjipotok Arboretum
The abstract sculptural quality of the garden's forms are highlighted in the early morning mist.

Volcjipotok Arboretum

The pyramidal form of the neighbouring hill has been used as a focus for the garden's design. Textural and tonal contrasts abound in the parterre between the hedges' dark solidity and the more natural textures of the infill plantings.

Opposite page:
Contrasting globose and columnar plant forms frame steps to the balustraded platform on which the house once stood.

Volcjipotok Arboretum
A pentagon of spherically-clipped box occupies the centre of one of the gardens adjoining the main parterre.

A Plague Cross, found in town squares and in the country throughout central Europe, was thought to act as a talisman or protection against plague.

Opposite page:
A weeping beech, Fagus sylvatica 'Pendula', has been given enough space to grow into its full natural form.

War II culminating in the public opening in 1956 of the Arboretum Volcjipotok near Llubljana. The original planting at Volcjipotok dates back to the seventeenth century and subsequent developments took place at the turn of this century when a grand Italianate parterre and a romantic landscape garden were made. But the main plantings of magnolias, rhododendrons and perennials around its series of lakes were not made until the period between World Wars I and II. In recent years, the plant collections in this 200-acre park have been further augmented with birch, Lawson cypress, lime, spruce, maple and juniper cultivars. Shrubs such as cotoneasters are featured as are perennials such as astilbes and primulas. Demonstration gardens and plant sales areas add to the arboretum's attractions.

Three years after Volcjipotok was opened to the public, the Dubrovnik botanic garden was founded for the purpose of studying and growing the sub-tropical succulent plants which thrive in Mediterranean climate. Situated on the island of Lokrum, the Dubrovnik garden uses the experimental plantings made by Austro-Hungarian Emperor Maximilian I as a basis for its five-acre collections, which now numbers over 1,500. The most recent botanic garden to be founded in Yugoslavia is at Skopje, the capital of Macedonia. Its thirty-five acres already contain a collection of over 1,500 taxa. It was at Vranja, near Skopje, that two of the best known trees of Yugoslav origin were discovered — the edible gage, *Cydonia 'Vranje'* and the golden-leaved beech *Fagus sylvatica 'Zlatia'*. The country's newest arboretum is at Lišičine near Zagreb, where the tree plantings have been organized on a geographical basis and there is a specialization on tree cultivars of Eastern and Central European origin.

Yugoslavia possesses a wide variety of botanic gardens which admirably represent the diverse climatic and topographical areas to be found in the country.

RUMANIA

Before 1859, the country of Rumania did not technically exist. In that year, Prince Ioaon Cuza was elected ruler of both Moldavia and Wallachia thus uniting these ancient principalities into one country. After World War I Transylvania, together with the smaller regions of the Banat, Maramures and Bucovina were transferred from Hungary to Rumania, thus giving the country its present political boundaries. Geographically and climatically, Rumania is divided into three regions by the huge horseshoe of the Carpathian mountains. The continental climate of Transylvania, a continuation of the Great Hungarian Plain, is less severe than that of Moldavia to the east where hot, dry summers are followed by devastatingly cold winters. Wallachia, which lies along the coastline of the Black Sea to the south, is milder enjoying a virtual Mediterranean climate.

Much of the Carpathian mountain area is covered by forest. The Mount Ceahlau nature reserve has a typical growth of beech, fir and spruce succeeded on higher ground by a lower scrub of dwarf pine, juniper and bilberry. There are many magnificent stands of larch to interest the tree lover, including a special reservation at Criminis. Wild flower enthusiasts will marvel at the famous Narcissus Glade at Sercaia where in late May or early June a whole hillside is covered with the blossom of poet's narcissus.

Of the Roman occupation which occurred in AD 105-106, only fragmentary mosaic pavements survive at Constanta on the Black Sea. However the poet Ovid exiled to this area by the Emperor Octavian Augustus, has left an account of life there at that time. No records of gardening survive for the subsequent Byzantine period but it may at least be assumed that simple plantings were made around monasteries. In 1369, with the arrival of the Turks in Wallachia, the gradual disruption of the Byzantine way of life began. A parallel invasion of Moldavia by Central European Tatars caused King Stephen the Great to build a series of vast fortress-monasteries controlling the valley-routes into the Carpathians. Moldovita, Sucevita and Dragomirna are the most impressive survivors of this period and it may be assumed that the orchards, kitchen gardens and woods surrounding them today are descendants of those under cultivation in the Middle Ages. In the beginning the mediaeval *boyars* or nobles of Rumania led a migratory life, never setting down long enough to establish permanent gardens. But gradually princely residences began to be built within the walls of fortified monasteries like Galata or Cetatuia or fortified towns like Iasi, then the capital of Moldavia. Early seventeenth-century chronicles describe groves of chestnuts, fruit trees and a rose garden growing between the princely palace and its church in the town of Tirgoviste, then the capital of Wallachia. This development culminated in the brief but glittering period of Constantin Brincoveaunu, Prince of Wallachia from 1688 to 1714. Symbol of the Rumanian Renaissance, the prince was one of the great amateur architect-builders in European history. Known for devising what is called the Brincovenesc architectural style — a curious mixture of Byzantine, Gothic and Venetian — Brincoveaunu laid out symmetrical terraces in formal and Renaissance style around his country houses at Potlogi (1698) and Mogosaia (1700-1702).

The seventeenth and eighteenth centuries were a period of great prosperity for Transylvania. It managed to maintain a degree of independance from the Ottoman Empire, while its ruling princes and officials cultivated close ties with the Austrian Empire. The elaborate Baroque style of gardening was flourishing in Austria under a prevailing French influence. In Transylvania the French taste was represented most fully in three gardens. Bontida, the seventeenth-century seat of the Banffy family, had a garden so elaborate it was know as the 'Transylvanian Versailles'. Avrig, the seat of Count Samuel Bruckenthal, an intimate of the Empress Maria Theresia and Governor of Transylvania until 1877 and Gornesti, the estate of the Teleki family, was given a garden in 1797. Soon after, Count Joseph Teleki, laid out an informal, natural landscape park around the formal garden at Gornesti. This was followed by similar parks in the region, created either around new houses such as at Savarsin, Chirales and Carei or around older houses and gardens as at Avrig and Bontida. Between 1824 and 1826 a Wallachian nobleman, Constantin Golescu, travelled throughout Austria, Switzerland and Rumania taking particular note of the many gardens and parks he saw in these countries, and his writings provide us with an invaluable source of information about their design and plantings. Golescu's own park, known as Belvedere, was located outside of Bucharest and is now lost.

When Wallachia and Moldavia were finally united under the new title of Rumania in 1859, both its first ruling prince, Ioaon Cuza, and its first president, Barbu Catargi, enjoyed informal landscape parks around their country residences. Cuza's, at Ruginoasa near Iasi, had a neo-Gothic house dating from 1811 as its centrepiece, unlike Catargi's at Maia in the Prakova valley which had a river winding under arched bridges and weeping willows, rockeries and Chinese pavilions all set against a background of wooded hills.

In 1881 the parliament, wanting a neutral outsider on the throne, offered it to the Prussian Prince Carol of Hohenzollern-Sigmaringen. Carol duly accepted and was crowned King Carol I. Two years later, he began a summer palace, park and garden at Sinaia in the Southern Carpathians. The assortment of architectural styles in the palace — German, English and Italian Renaissance, Baroque, Rococo and Hispano-Moorish — was matched by an equally varied assortment of ornamental features in the park — terraces, flight of steps, bridges, loggias and cascades, all disposed apparently at random rather than in one coherent scheme. An eclectic collection of conifers made up the planting in the park. Sinaia thus embodies important developments in late nineteenth-century garden design — an interest in historicism on the one hand and in making botanical collections on the other. Another prime example of the passion for things past so in vogue at the time was the Bibesco family's restoration of the house of their ancestor Prince Constantin Brincoveaunu at Mogasaia, while the period's botanical enthusiasm was further evidenced by the foundation of two important arboreta. Simeria was the creation of Count Glai and Zam which was the work of Michael Czarnovitz, who collected tree species around the world and particularly in the Himalayas and Patagonia. Botanic gardens were also established in Iasi (1856) by the amateur naturalist Dr Anastasie Fatu, in Bucharest (1860) by the university and at Cluj by Count Miko. The contemporaneous city park movement, propelled by the dramatic enlargement of cities, is represented best in Rumania by the Cismigui Park in Bucharest, which was developed in the 1830s to the design of the German landscape gardener Carl F.W. Meyer. Meyer was the first of a succession of foreign landscape designers to work on the gardens and parks of Rumania — a succession which also included another German, F. von Rehbun, the Belgian, L. Fuchs, designer of the Belgian gardens of Beervelde and Hanzinelle as well as two Frenchmen, Pinard and Edouard Redont (the latter's theory of gardening as a Social Art had an important input in late nineteenth-century France).

In England around this time a reaction set in against the grandeur and apparently directionless eclecticism of nineteenth-century garden design, favoring instead a return to the basic principles of simple planting and honest craftmanship. In 1897 the English Queen Marie of Rumania, wife of Ferdinand I, commissioned M.H. Baillie Scott (1865-1945), one of the principal adherents of this new movement, to build a tree-house in the park at Sinaia. She also laid out a garden in this new Arts-and-Crafts style at Balcic on the shores of the Black Sea. The simplicity of style characteristic of the period led in due course to what in gardening as well as in the other arts is known as the Modern movement. The most outstanding monument of this period is at the park at Tirgu Mures which was designed by the sculptor Constantin Brancusi as a memorial to the Rumanian victims of World War I.

In Rumania the Japanese influence is best represented by the section of the Cluj-Napoca Botanic Garden designed by Professor Borza in the 1920s. The post World War II period saw the establishment of many botanic gardens in Rumania. One was founded at Craiova in 1953, while that at Iasi was relocated in 1963. Another was set up at Sibiu as a teaching centre in 1968 on the initiative of Professor Vasille Fatu. In 1826 Constantin Golescu wrote of the difficulty of establishing a garden in Rumania, whose geographical position at the crossroads of great empires brought about frequent destruction at the hands of invading armies. Nonetheless, an unexpectedly large number of gardens and parks representing many periods of gardening survive in the country today.

Majlath Castle
The late nineteenth-century neo-Baroque Italianate staircase.

CLUJ-NAPOCA,
UNIVERSITY BOTANIC GARDEN

Gornesti
The natural park around the Baroque mansion was laid out by Count Joseph Teleki.

Cluj-Napoca
One of the richest botanic gardens in central Europe. It began as a public park laid out towards the end of the nineteenth century by Count Miko and presented to the city.

All but enclosed by the Carpathian mountains, the province of Transylvania extends in a rolling upland plateau between peaks which are sometimes gaunt and forbidding and at others friendly, green and inviting. It a country rich in mythic atmosphere — with a unique and fascinating history well-known as the setting for Bram Stoker's novel 'Dracula'. Its difficult terrain spared it from the Turkish domination which plagued the surrounding plains for several centuries, while its unique ethnic mix of Rumanians, Hungarians and Saxons has given it an exceptional cultural diversity.

It was during the period that it was part of the Austro-Hungarian Empire that Transylvania's principal parks and gardens were created, often by imperial governors or other officials, Count Samuel Bruckenthal, left the province two important legacies: his palace in the town of Sibiu which includes the oldest and finest art collection in Rumania, and his country house and garden at nearby Avrig. The house was built in 1763 and the fourteen-acre formal garden was laid out five years later. Its terraces — some retained by cut stone walls, others by grass banks — are linked by magnificent flights of balustraded steps, fountains, jets, rivulets and cascades which lead down into alleys lined with carefully-shorn trees. By the time Constantin Golescu visited the garden around 1825, an informal romantic park had been added with a bark house and sham Roman ruins modelled on the ones which had been built in the royal garden at Schönbrunn in 1778.

Also to be seen at the house at this time were an important collection of fruit trees with 95 pear, 45 peach and 17 apple varieties, an orangerie, and greenhouses with almost 1,000 orange and lemon trees and a variety of palms and opuntias. Bruckenthal's patronage of horticulture led to the naming of a native heath-like shrub, *Bruckenthalia spiculifolia*, in his honour. Flower culture predominated in the middle of nineteenth century with the narcissus, primula, carnation, pelargonium, verbena, violet and the rose being grown in quantity. In 1873 the family exchanged the property for one in Vienna and Avrig became a sanatorium, in which use it continues today. The garden is still in good condition with many of its ornamental features intact. Cool fountains and refreshing streams remain an important feature with their banks planted with flowering shrubs, perennials and an excellent display of summer-flowering annuals. The park also remains in good condition with avenues of chestnut, lime, hornbeam, oak, spruce and juniper. Smaller alleys of lilac and box have fine individual specimens of tulip tree, magnolia, catalpa and yew scattered among them.

The Teleki family also left Transylvania a twin legacy: the Teleki library in Tirgu Mures with its treasury of manuscripts, incunabulae and early printed books and the nearby country house and garden of Gornesti. Count Joseph Teleki became a friend and partisan of Jean-Jacques Rousseau during his travels in France. In 1760 he published *Essai sur la Faiblesse*

des Esprits Forts, a defense of Rousseau against his rival Voltaire. On his return to Transylvania he laid out a formal park at Gornesti with interlocking canals, pools and elaborate scroll parterres decorated with grotesque stone sculptures representing figures from the French Revolution such as Louis XVI, Mirabeau and Les Dames des Halles in dwarf form. Around this he later created a romantic landscape park, the chief feature of which was an immense lake surrounding the house on three sides and planted along its banks with willow, oak, maple, birch, poplar and pine. His achievement can be judged in an 1818 painting by Joseph Neuhauser and an 1857 lithograph by Rohbock. The Teleki family also boasts a botanical genus named in its honour, the principal member of which is a yellow ox-eyed daisy, *Telekia speciosa*.

The Banffy family was settled for many centuries around the town of Cluj, where their eighteenth-century palace now houses an art gallery. Their country house, Bontida, gradually developed its present form through successive rebuilding over the course of years. In the seventeenth century it was surrounded by a formal Baroque garden and in 1830 an English garden was laid out with the technical assistance of an engineer from Cluj and decorated with romantic garden structures including a *tempietto* and an hermitage in neo-Gothic style; the house was later transformed in the same style.

The last of the great Transylvanian families to create a landscape park were the Bethlens whose influence reached a peak in 1608 when Gorinal Bethlen promoted himself from governor to Prince of Transylvania. Between 1810 and 1813, Count Lajos Bethlen built a new house at the family seat and surrounded it with an English garden decorated with mythological statues carved by the Viennese sculptor Schmitzer. Smaller parks were created in other parts of the region, among them Sarasvin and Carei. Both were laid out by Hungarian-based designer, C.H. Nebbien and Gyog Bode respectively. Considering the close ties which existed between the two areas since the eleventh century it is not surprising that the predilection for the informal landscape park which was strong in Hungary in the early nineteenth century eventually spilled over into Transylvania.

The University Garden at Cluj-Napoca, an important city in the centre of Transylvania, is among the richest and most attractively laid out of its kind in Central Europe. Beginning in the nineteenth century as a public park donated to the city

Cluj-Napoca
The garden was established as a botanic garden in 1920 under Professor Borza who laid out the Japanese garden.

Traditional raised Japanese stepping stones, to allow dry passage for slippered feet over wet ground.

by Count Miko, it was established in 1920 as a botanic garden under Professor Borza, who remained its director until 1947. Its undulating ground form was broken with collection of trees and two areas of distinct thematic design, the Japanese Garden and the Classical Roman Garden.

Towards the end of the nineteenth century Eastern culture began to exercise a profound influence on the West, not least in the field of landscape gardening. In 1893 Joseph Conder, an English architect living in Japan, published his *Landscape Gardening in Japan.* Illustrated with excellent photographs and diagrams, it presented the ancient gardens of Japan to the Western world for the first time. Soon afterwards the first Japanese-style gardens were created in the West. The famous Japanese Tea Garden in Golden Gate Park, San Francisco was made in 1894. The first decade of the new century saw important examples made at Tatton Park in England, Tully in Ireland and in the Jardin Albert Kahn in Paris. Since then, the Japanese-style garden has been a recurrent sub-theme in twentieth-century gardening in the West. Only two such gardens exist in Central Europe; one is at the Cluj-Napoca Botanic Garden, while the other is in the Freedom Park in Sofia, Bulgaria. The late nineteenth century also saw a revival of interest in the gardens of classical Rome — not in monumental creations, such as Hadrian's Villa near Tivoli, which had been the focus for previous Classical revivals — but rather in the small, intimately-scaled gardens or courtyards of town houses like those excavated at Pompeii. The Rumanians had a particular interest in this revival on account of their Roman ancestry.

The Japanese water garden with an island and tea house in the background.

SINAIA

Sinaia Palace
The light-filled parterre, decorated with flower-filled urns, is effectively contrasted with the sombre conifer woodlands behind.

Opposite page:
A fountain-screen with figures of Neptune and other sea-gods delicately-clothed in a single-coloured scheme of orange-yellow flowers. (All photographs of Sinaia by Margaret Rutherford)

The southernmost range of the Carpathian mountains is known as the Bucegi Massif. Here green valleys are bounded by rugged mountain peaks. Caves and river gorges are succeeded on higher ground by dense forests of beech, spruce and fir, which further up give way to rolling alpine meadows. The area is home to a population of birds and beasts of prey — vultures and eagles, lynx, bear and wolf — that today is sadly diminishing despite the area's status as a natural reserve. In one of the narrow wooded valleys stands a monastery, its church Sinaia dating from 1695 is called after both the Mount and the Desert in the Holy Land. When King Carol I and his wife first chose Sinaia as their place for summer residence, they stayed in the monastery while the construction of their palace took place on a shady slope above. The palace is a kind of tropical Balmoral in a German Gothic style with Byzantine and Renaissance features. Set in a sloping park cut out of the surrounding forest, it stands above a great amphitheatre of stone terraces with assorted flights of steps, bridges, ornament and parterres. Smaller palaces such as Foisor, a forty-roomed hunting lodge, and Pelosor, built between 1899 and 1903 for the heir to the throne, add to the variety of the overall park complex.

The royal gardens reached their peak under the direction of the English Queen Marie, granddaughter of Queen Victoria and wife of Ferdinand I. She lightened many of the park's ponderous architectural features by superimposing light iron pergolas festooned with climbing plants. She also brightened the view from the house by creating a series of flower-gardens that function as islands of colour within the predominant greens of the conifer-planted park. Her guests were frequently treated to picnics in a tree-house built high in a cluster of pines and reached by a rope-ladder. The structure was designed by the English Arts-and-Crafts architect W.H.Baillie Scott

(1865-1945), whose light, airy and beautifully-crafted houses were a popular antidote to the solemn and gloomy architecture typical of the period. Scott was convinced that house and garden should have the same designer in order to ensure an overall, integrated environment — a proposition he advanced in two books, *Houses and Gardens* (1906) and *Garden Suburbs* (1910). As popular in the German-speaking world as he was in his native England, Scott provided schemes for the Grand Ducal Palace in Darmstadt (1897), for Queen Marie's sister and for the Landhaus Waldbuhl house and garden in Switzerland. The gradual relaxation of court life also led to Queen Maries's construction of a seaside villa in a curious partly Moorish style at Balcic (now in Bulgaria) on the Riviera-like coast of the Black Sea. Her garden of paved courts, lily ponds and dry stone walls seems to have come from the pages of *The Studio* magazine, the bible of the Art-and-Crafts movement which began publishing in London in 1893. Later, as Queen Mother, she restored the early seventeenth-century castle of Bran near Sinai to function as a summer house. There she was visited by the English writer Sacheverell Sitwell, who in his *Rumanian Journeys* (1938) described her orchard of apple trees planted in the water meadows below the castle and her beautiful flower garden. The latter boasted a famous collection of dahlias numbering over 200 varieties, mostly of English and German origin.

Sinaia is just one of a chain of romantic summer houses and gardens built all over Europe during the nineteenth century by Kings and Royal Consorts of German origin. Along with Balmoral Castle in Scotland, Pena Castle and Buçaco in Portugal, Stara Zagora in Bulgaria and many others, it is an eloquent expression of royal European taste in architecture and gardening during this period.

CITY PARKS AND BOTANIC GARDENS
Bucharest

Herastrau Park
The park was laid out during the 1920's by the French designer, Pinard, for an international exhibition. (Photograph by Margaret Rutherford)

Opposite page, top:
The principal attraction of the park today is the assembly of nearly 300 rural Rumanian buildings.

Opposite page, below:
Potlogi Palace
The Palace was built in 1698 by the Prince of Wallachia, Constandin Brincoveaunu. Its garden was re-erected at the beginning of this century in light-filled, impressionistic design. The dappled shadows thrown by the vine-wreathed cast-iron pergola. (Photograph by Margaret Rutherford)

Cotroceni
A stone pergola overlooks a garden devoted to a variety of perennial flowering plants. The garden was created by Queen Marie, wife of King Ferdinand I, in her native English style. (Photograph by Margaret Rutherford)

Bucharest is a spacious capital crowded with parks, avenues of plane trees and scattered lakes. The lakes are fed by the innumerable streams flowing down from the Southern Carpathians to join the Danube or from one of the marshes which ring the city. In excessively hot summers the people of the city take refuge in the parks where iced drinks, sherbets and rustic suppers are served to the accompaniment of music. Cismigiu, the first of these parks to be created, was laid out by the German landscape gardener Carl F.W. Meyer in the 1830s, when over 30,000 trees and shrubs were positioned around a reed-fringed lake. In 1910 the park was redesigned by another German landscape architect F. von Rehbun, in a mixture of formal and romantic styles. Today long rows of clipped lime trees, yew hedges, rose gardens and box-edged beds filled with seasonal bedding provide a basic structure. A circular lawn decorated with busts of Rumanian writers serves to educate its visitors about the country's past.

Cotroceni, the second park to be made, was developed towards the end of the nineteenth century around the monastery from which it derives its name. In 1874 part of it was given over to the relocated Bucharest Botanic Garden, the new layout for which was completed in 1891 by the Belgian designer L. Fuchs. The remainder of the park was, like the Cismigiu, designed by von Rehbun. The monastery was later used by the future King Ferdinand I and his English wife, Queen Marie, as their city residence. With the assistance of the French garden designer, Julius Janine, who also laid out the garden at Balcic on the Black Sea, the garden at Cotroceni

was redesigned, with flower-filled terraces, pergolas and balustrades wreathed in vines, ivies and wisteria.

During the 1920s Rehbun also designed the layout of Herastrau Park on the shores of Lake Herastrau in the northern part of the city, assisted this time by a Frenchman called Pinard. Today the enormous park — about 500 acres — remains mostly in the form of a natural landscape of water and islands planted with willow and poplar. Its principal attractions are an assembly of nearly 300 Rumanian rural buildings that function as a Village Museum and the annual flower show, known as Expoflora. Other parks include

Cismigiu Park

Recently landscaped areas of the park are characterized by austere essays in geometric paving as exemplified in this summer flower garden. First laid out in the 1830's, it was redesigned in 1910 by the German garden designer, F. von Rehbun, in a mixture of formal and romantic styles. Today a lawn decorated with busts of famous Rumanian writers fulfil one of a public park's traditional roles — that of public education.

Kiseleff, located on Soseaua Kiseleff, the most grandiose of Bucharest's leafy avenues, and Liberty Park in the southern part of the city with its hyperbolic marble arch celebrating Rumania's liberation from centuries of Ottoman rule.

Outside of the city along the valley of the Dombovita river — a tributary of the Danube on which Bucharest is built — are Mogosaia and Potlogi, two country houses built by Constantin Brincoveaunu during his tragically-brief reign as Prince of Wallachia from 1688 to 1714. Mogosaia is situated on the banks of a lake formed by the river Colentina amidst a landscape of beautiful trees, vast meadows and distant hills. Built by Venetians who came through Dalmatia to work for Prince Constantin, the property lay neglected after the prince and his four sons were beheaded in Constantinople in 1714. In 1870 a descendant of Prince Constantin, Prince Nicolas Bibesco, began its restoration employing a French gardener called Montigny, who had previously worked at Versailles, to help him with the park. The long, straight, double avenue of horse chestnuts which leads from the park gate to the palace dates from his period. The restoration was continued by Princess Marthe Bibesco, who with the assistance of a Venetian architect, Domenico Rupolo, and his Rumanian colleague Georges Cantacuzene, completed the restoration of the house and formal terraces descending to the lake. These were planted with massed petunias in privet-edged beds while a pair of Byzantine stone lions in an archaic style brought from the family house in Bucharest was set up to guard the central flight of steps. The lake was filled with colonies of water lilies and its margins covered with immense group of iris. Laburnum walks still open to reveal groves of lilac and in a secret walled garden periwinkles, violets, lilies of the valley and jasmine scent the air. Along with nearby Potlogi, which was built just two years before Mogosaia but had to wait until the 1960s for its restoration, both places still give the visitor a vivid taste of the atmosphere of the all-to-brief Rumanian Renaissance.

TIRGU JIU, Public Park

The Gate of the Kiss has incised
decoration incorporating
Constantin Brancusi's famous
'Kiss' motif in the upright piers.

The Table of Silence, the circular slab surrounded by twelve monolithic stone seats, represents the empty places at many Rumanian dining tables as a result of World War I.

The Womens' Association of Gorj — the native province of the great Rumanian sculptor Constantin Brancusi (1876-1957) — invited him to create a World War I memorial park in the town of Tirgu Jiu. Brancusi felt that his monumental abstract sculptures needed to be shown in the neutral setting of a public park. In such a position, several pieces could be set so as to give, both in themselves and in relation to each other, a spiritual or emotive meaning to their environment. In response to the association request, Brancusi designed a set of three monumental pieces — the 'Table of Silence' 'The Gate of the Kiss' and 'The Endless Column' — to be aligned along a mile-long axis in the town. The first two were to be located in the public park, and the last at a point to the east in the town. The axis thus created has been likened to that created by a similar trinity of elements in the heart of Paris: the large circular flower bed in the gardens of the Louvre, the Arc du Carousel and the obelisk in the Place de la Concorde. Brancusi's work is remarkable for the way in which it combines an uncompromising modern abstraction with the forms of native Rumanian folk art. Nowhere is this synthesis more apparent than at Tirgu Jiu. 'The Table of Silence' — a circular stone slab surrounded by twelve monolithic stone stools — abstractly suggests the empty spaces at a family dining table.

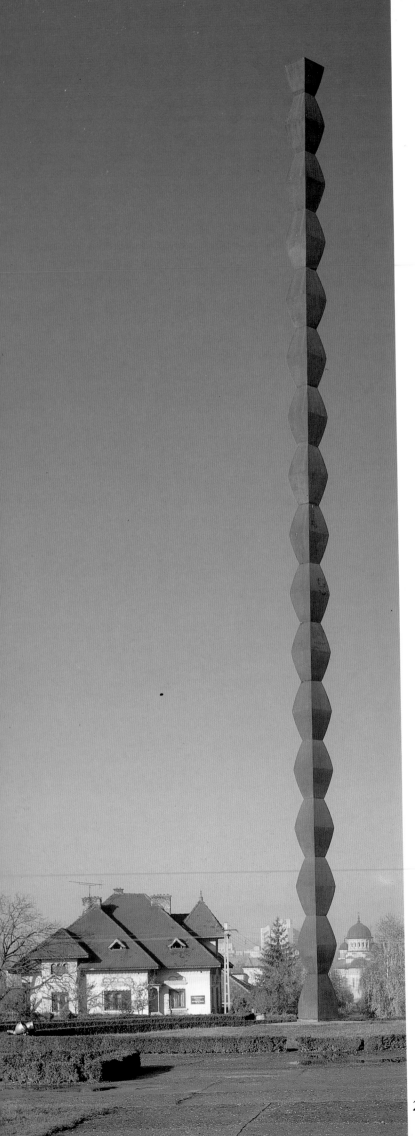

The 'Table' also suggests round tables of wood or stone frequently found in Rumanian cottages used for display of offerings during funeral services in church courtyards.

'The Gate of the Kiss' similarly bridges the forms of modern abstract art and Rumanian folkart conventions, both in its overall shape and in the incised linear decoration with which it is covered. Though its form is reminiscent of the Western tradition of the monumental arch it is closer in scale to the traditional, carved farmhouse gates of the surrounding countryside. 'The Endless Column', the third and most memorable element in the ensemble, is a 100-foot high cast iron structure composed of a series of superimposed truncated pyramids alternately residing base-to-base and apex-to-apex. Pyramids and obelisks play a large part in the burial or funerary structures of the Western tradition, yet here they are incorporated into an overall form which relates as well to the carved wooden death-poles which in south-west Rumania are placed over the graves of young men.

Although Brancusi left Rumania at the age of twenty-seven and lived in Paris for the remainder of his life, he remained emotionally and spiritually tied to the folk-forms of his native country's art. Tirgu Jiu is an eminent example of the synthesis this artist managed to achieve between these two sources of inspiration.

Tirgu Jiu
The Endless Column, pictured with the town of Tirgu Jiu in the background to show the scale of Brancusi's sculpture. Detail of the Endless Column, the 100-foot high cast-iron structure is composed of a series of superimposed truncated pyramids alternately residing base-to-base and apex-to-apex.

INDEX

BIBLIOGRAPHY

General

BASSETT, Richard. *A Guide to Central Europe* (London), 1987.
Balkan Hours (London), 1990
FERMOR, Patrick Leigh. *A Time of Gifts* (London), 1977
HOBHOUSE, Penelope; TAYLOR, Patrick; Editors. *The Gardens of Europe* (London), 1990
JELLICOE, Sir Geoffrey; JELLICOE, Susan; GOODE, Patrick; Lancaster, Michael; Editors. *The Oxford Companion to Gardens* (Oxford, New York), 1986
KNOX, Brian. *Baroque Architecture in Central Europe* (London), 1966
LYALL, Archibald. *The Balkan Road* (London), 1930
MAGRIS, Claudio. *Danube* (London), 1989
SITWELL, Sacheverell. *Great Palaces* (London), 1964

East Germany

BADAR, Regina; BRUCKSCH, Ekkehard; MROSKO, Astrid; RIPPL, Helmut. *Der Muskauer Park* (Bad Muskau), 1987
BOETTIGER, Carl August. *Reise nash Wörlitz* (Wörlitz), 1988
KOHLSCHMIDT, Siegfried; HARTEL, Ricardo. *Schloss und Park Branitz* (Dresden), 1988
KOHN, Alex R. *Schlösser und Gärten um Worlitz* (Leipzig), 1990
NEIDHARDT, Hans Joachim. *Schloss Pillnitz* (Dresden), 1988

Poland

DIALOBOK, Stefan. «Trees and Schrubs of some Parks in Poland», in *I.D.S. Year Book* (London) 1970
CZARTORYSKA, Isabelle. *Thoughts on the Manner of Planting Gardens* (Wroclaw), 1804
JAROSZEWSKI, Tadeusz S. *The Book of Warsaw Palaces* (Warsaw), 1984
KNOX, Brian. *Architecture in Poland* (London), 1971
PEVSNER, N. «The Landscape Garden in Poland, Bohemia» in *The Picturesque Garden outside The British Isles* (Washington), 1974
PIWKOWSKI, Wlodzimierz. *Nieborów Arkadia* (Warsaw), 1988
SHARMAN, Tim. *Poland* (London), 1988
SITWELL, Sacheverell. «A Palace in Poland, Lazieńki Warsaw», in *Country Life* (London), 4 June 1938
WARD, Philip. *Polish Cities* (Cambridge, New York), 1988

Czechoslovakia

ČAPEK, Karel. *The Gardener's Year* (London), 1931
ČIHAŘ, Martin. *Přírodní Brásy Českoslovenka* (Prague), 1989
FRASER, Hedvika. «Gardens and Gardening behind the Iron Curtain», in *Hortus* (Rhayader) N.° 10 Summer 1989
GALANDAVER, Jan; KUSÁK, Dalibor. *Konopiště* (Prague), 1988
KUSÁK, Dalibor. *Lednice* (Prague), 1986
KUSÁK, Dalibor; BURIAN, Jiři, KRIŽANOVÁ, Muchka, Ivan. *Hrady a Zámky v Československu* (Prague), 1990
McCLINTOCK, David. «Tour in Czechoslovakia and Hungary», in *I.D.S. Year Book* (London), 1988
PROKOP, Paul; HOŘEJŠÍ, Jiřira. *Morava Umělecké Památky* (Prague) 1986
REDAKCE, Hlavní. *Hrady, Zámky Atvrze v Čechách, na Moravé a ve Slezsku* (Prague), 1988
WOOD, J. «Tour in Czechoslovakia» in *I.D.S. Year Book* (London), 1986

Hungary

KELÉNYI, György. *Kastélyok, Kúriák, Villák* (Budapest), 1974
KRISZT, György. *Nagycenk Széchenyi — Kastély* (Budapest) 1990
JOLÁN, Bak *Fertöd Esterházy Kastély* (Budapest), 1988
NEHRING, Dorothee. «The Landscape Architect, Christian Heinrich Nebbien and his Design for the Municipal Park in Budapest», in *Journal of Garden History* (London), Vol. 5, No. 3, July-Sept. 1985
ORSI, Károly. *Mansions in Hungary* (Budapest), 1990
STROKES, Adrian. *Hungary* (London), 1909
ZADOR, Anna. «The English Garden in Hungary» in *The Picturesque Garden and its Influence outside the British Isles* (Washington), 1974

Yugoslavia

IVANČEVIĆ, R. *Art Treasures of Croatia* (Belgrade), 1986
KINDERSLEY, Anne. *The Mountains of Serbia* (London), 1976
UGRENOVIÉ, Alexandar. *Trsteno* (Zagreb), 1953

Rumania

GIURESÇU, Dinu C. *The Razing of Rumania's Past* (London), 1990
PATMORE, Derek. «A Country House in Rumania — The Palace of Mogosea», in *Country Life* (London) 6 Apr. 1940
SITWELL, Sacheverell. *Rumanian, Journeys,* (London), 1939